# UNITED!
## THE COMIC STRIP HISTORY

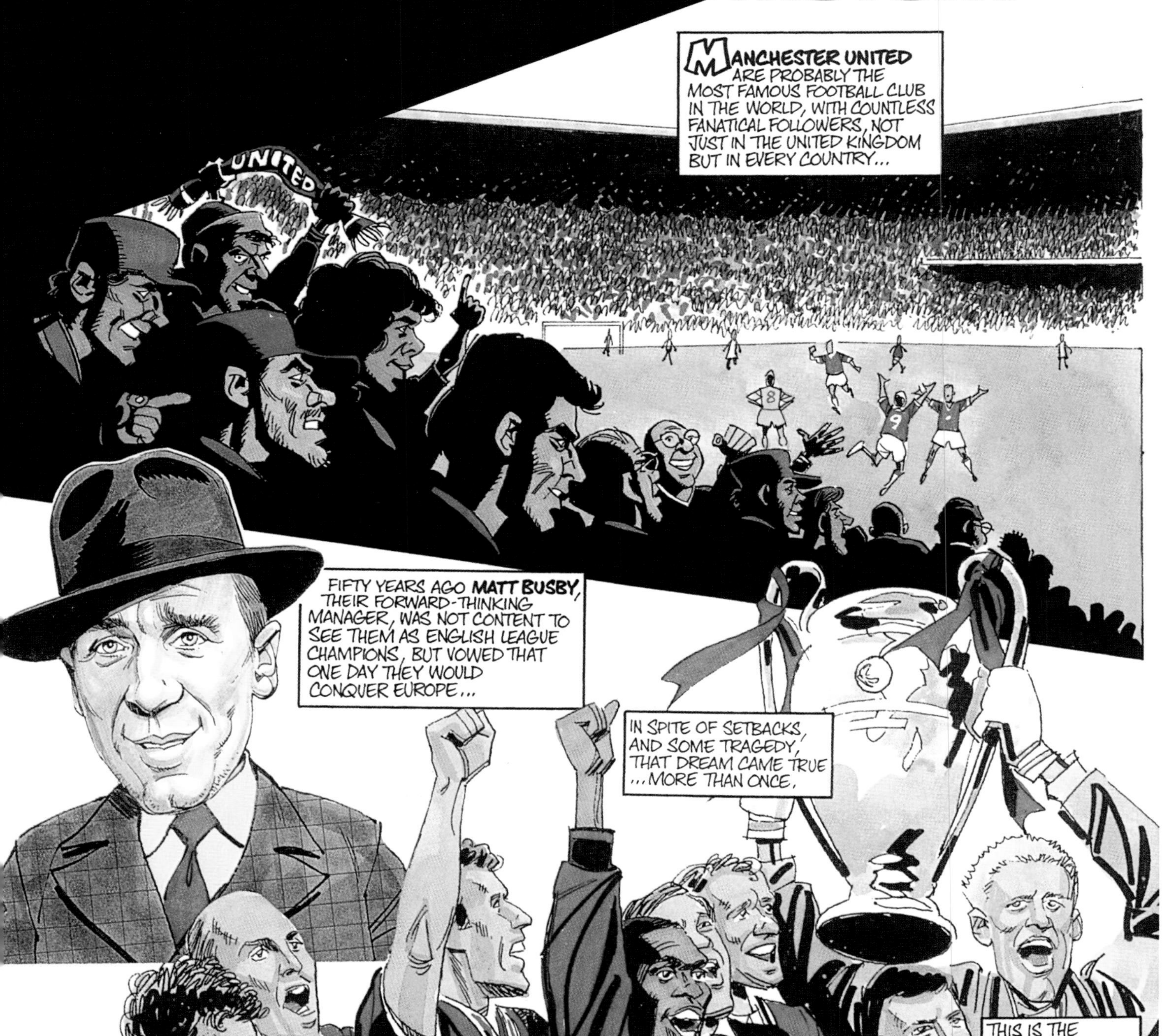
MANCHESTER UNITED ARE PROBABLY THE MOST FAMOUS FOOTBALL CLUB IN THE WORLD, WITH COUNTLESS FANATICAL FOLLOWERS, NOT JUST IN THE UNITED KINGDOM BUT IN EVERY COUNTRY...
UNITED
FIFTY YEARS AGO MATT BUSBY, THEIR FORWARD-THINKING MANAGER, WAS NOT CONTENT TO SEE THEM AS ENGLISH LEAGUE CHAMPIONS, BUT VOWED THAT ONE DAY THEY WOULD CONQUER EUROPE...
IN SPITE OF SETBACKS, AND SOME TRAGEDY, THAT DREAM CAME TRUE ...MORE THAN ONCE.
THIS IS THE GRAPHIC STORY OF MANCHESTER UNITED, OF TWO GREAT MANAGERS, OF WONDERFUL PLAYERS, AND OF MANY MEMORABLE ACHIEVEMENTS...

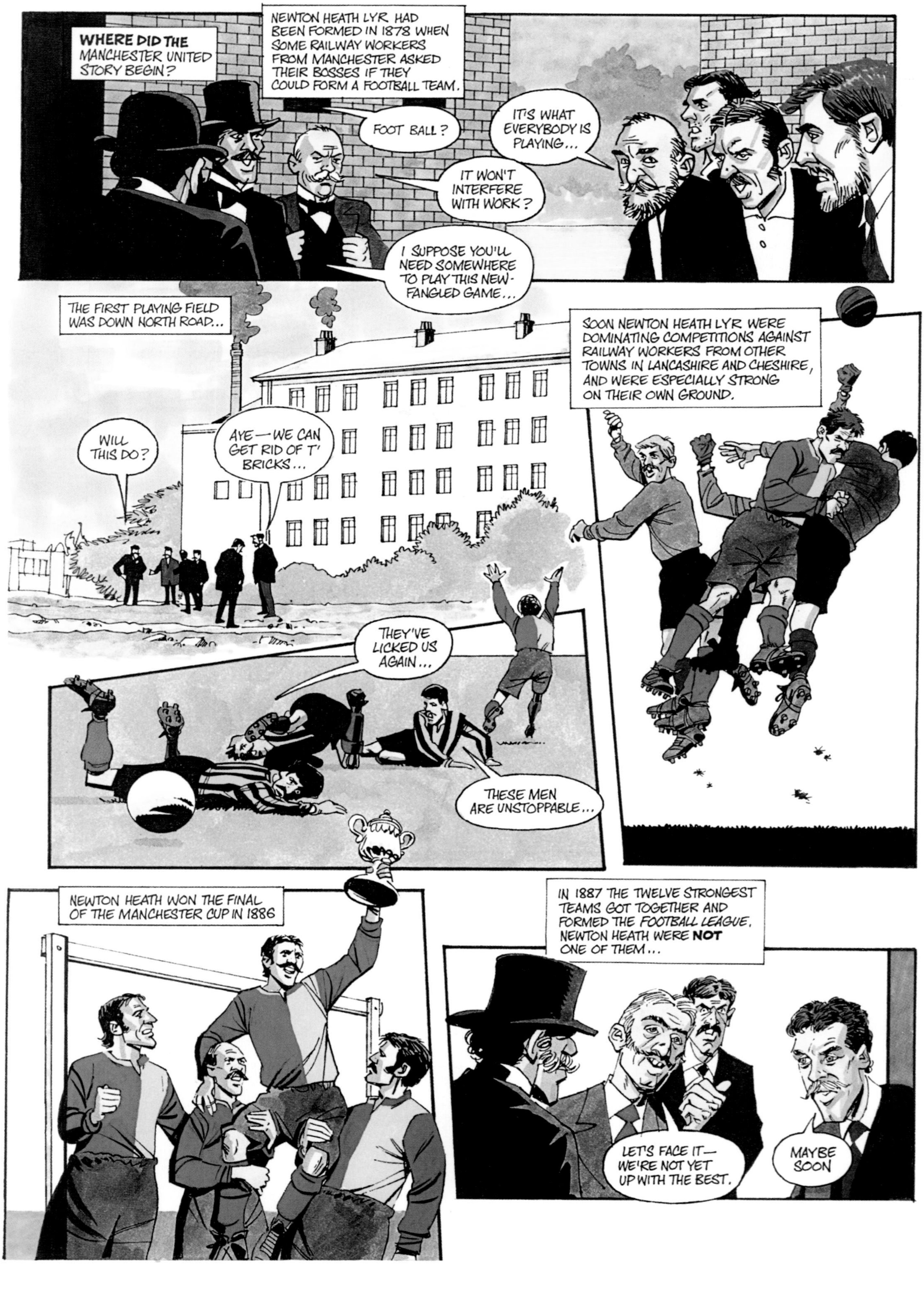
WHERE DID THE MANCHESTER UNITED STORY BEGIN?
NEWTON HEATH LYR HAD BEEN FORMED IN 1878 WHEN SOME RAILWAY WORKERS FROM MANCHESTER ASKED THEIR BOSSES IF THEY COULD FORM A FOOTBALL TEAM.
FOOT BALL?
IT'S WHAT EVERYBODY IS PLAYING...
IT WON'T INTERFERE WITH WORK?
I SUPPOSE YOU'LL NEED SOMEWHERE TO PLAY THIS NEW-FANGLED GAME...
THE FIRST PLAYING FIELD WAS DOWN NORTH ROAD...
WILL THIS DO?
AYE — WE CAN GET RID OF T' BRICKS...
SOON NEWTON HEATH LYR WERE DOMINATING COMPETITIONS AGAINST RAILWAY WORKERS FROM OTHER TOWNS IN LANCASHIRE AND CHESHIRE, AND WERE ESPECIALLY STRONG ON THEIR OWN GROUND.
THEY'VE LICKED US AGAIN...
THESE MEN ARE UNSTOPPABLE...
NEWTON HEATH WON THE FINAL OF THE MANCHESTER CUP IN 1886
IN 1887 THE TWELVE STRONGEST TEAMS GOT TOGETHER AND FORMED THE FOOTBALL LEAGUE. NEWTON HEATH WERE NOT ONE OF THEM...
LET'S FACE IT — WE'RE NOT YET UP WITH THE BEST.
MAYBE SOON

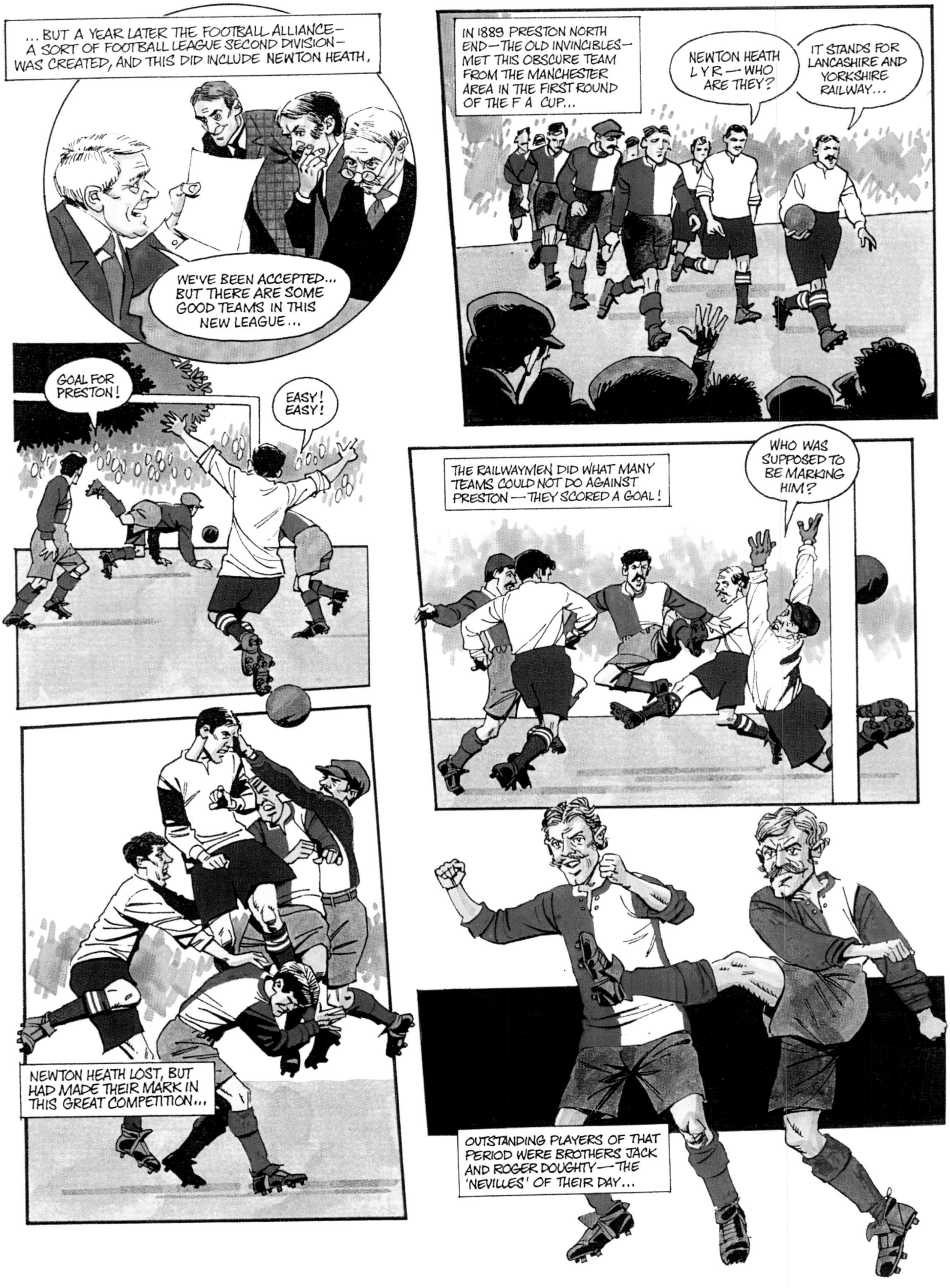
... BUT A YEAR LATER THE FOOTBALL ALLIANCE - A SORT OF FOOTBALL LEAGUE SECOND DIVISION - WAS CREATED, AND THIS DID INCLUDE NEWTON HEATH,
WE'VE BEEN ACCEPTED... BUT THERE ARE SOME GOOD TEAMS IN THIS NEW LEAGUE...
IN 1889 PRESTON NORTH END — THE OLD INVINCIBLES — MET THIS OBSCURE TEAM FROM THE MANCHESTER AREA IN THE FIRST ROUND OF THE F A CUP...
NEWTON HEATH L Y R — WHO ARE THEY?
IT STANDS FOR LANCASHIRE AND YORKSHIRE RAILWAY...
GOAL FOR PRESTON!
EASY! EASY!
THE RAILWAYMEN DID WHAT MANY TEAMS COULD NOT DO AGAINST PRESTON — THEY SCORED A GOAL!
WHO WAS SUPPOSED TO BE MARKING HIM?
NEWTON HEATH LOST, BUT HAD MADE THEIR MARK IN THIS GREAT COMPETITION...
OUTSTANDING PLAYERS OF THAT PERIOD WERE BROTHERS JACK AND ROGER DOUGHTY — THE 'NEVILLES' OF THEIR DAY...

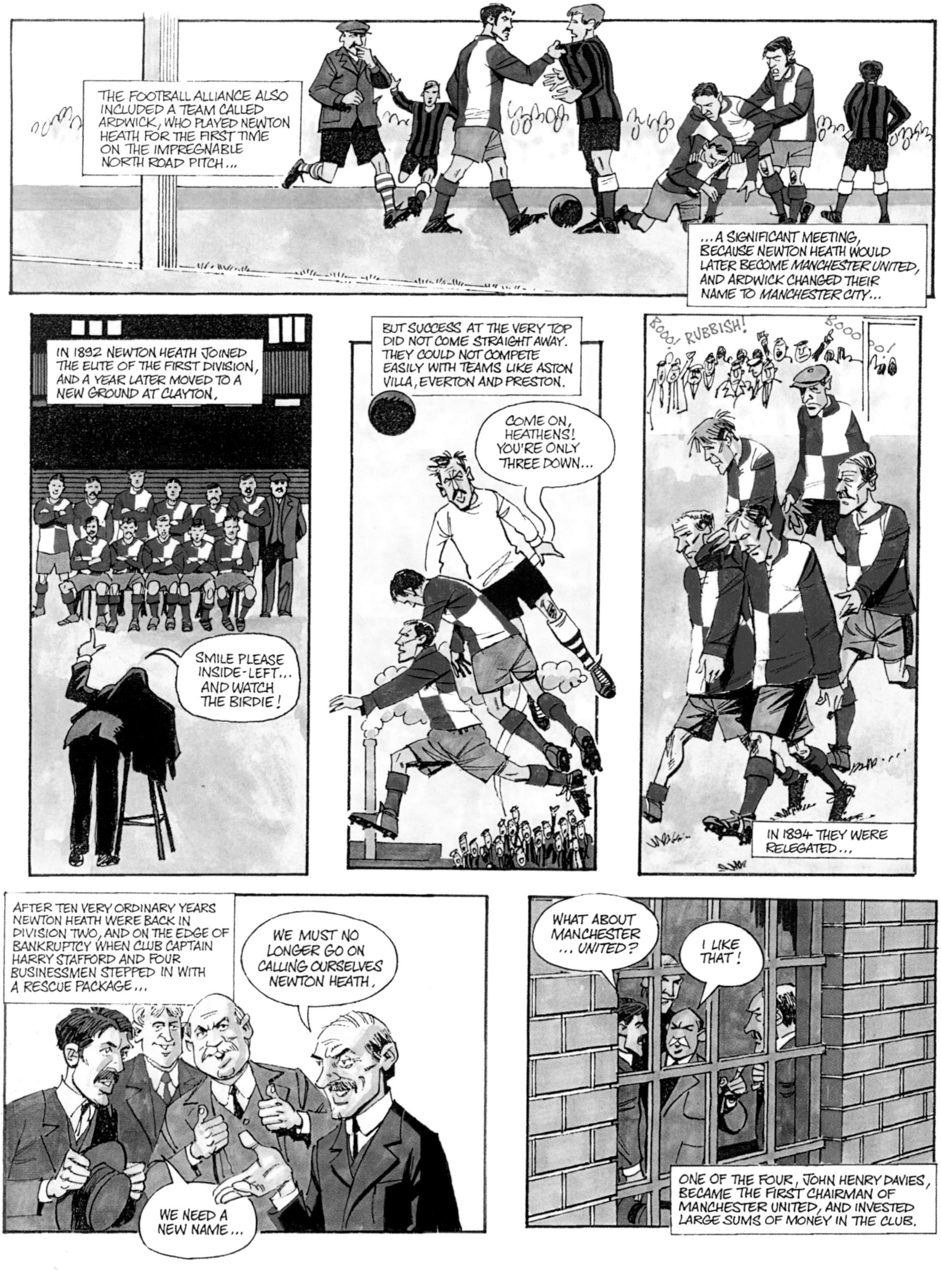
THE FOOTBALL ALLIANCE ALSO INCLUDED A TEAM CALLED ARDWICK, WHO PLAYED NEWTON HEATH FOR THE FIRST TIME ON THE IMPREGNABLE NORTH ROAD PITCH...
...A SIGNIFICANT MEETING, BECAUSE NEWTON HEATH WOULD LATER BECOME *MANCHESTER UNITED*, AND ARDWICK CHANGED THEIR NAME TO *MANCHESTER CITY*...
IN 1892 NEWTON HEATH JOINED THE ELITE OF THE FIRST DIVISION, AND A YEAR LATER MOVED TO A NEW GROUND AT CLAYTON.
SMILE PLEASE INSIDE-LEFT... AND WATCH THE BIRDIE!
BUT SUCCESS AT THE VERY TOP DID NOT COME STRAIGHT AWAY. THEY COULD NOT COMPETE EASILY WITH TEAMS LIKE ASTON VILLA, EVERTON AND PRESTON.
COME ON, HEATHENS! YOU'RE ONLY THREE DOWN...
BOOO! RUBBISH!
BOOO OO!
IN 1894 THEY WERE RELEGATED...
AFTER TEN VERY ORDINARY YEARS NEWTON HEATH WERE BACK IN DIVISION TWO, AND ON THE EDGE OF BANKRUPTCY WHEN CLUB CAPTAIN HARRY STAFFORD AND FOUR BUSINESSMEN STEPPED IN WITH A RESCUE PACKAGE...
WE MUST NO LONGER GO ON CALLING OURSELVES NEWTON HEATH.
WE NEED A NEW NAME...
WHAT ABOUT MANCHESTER ... UNITED?
I LIKE THAT!
ONE OF THE FOUR, JOHN HENRY DAVIES, BECAME THE FIRST CHAIRMAN OF MANCHESTER UNITED, AND INVESTED LARGE SUMS OF MONEY IN THE CLUB.

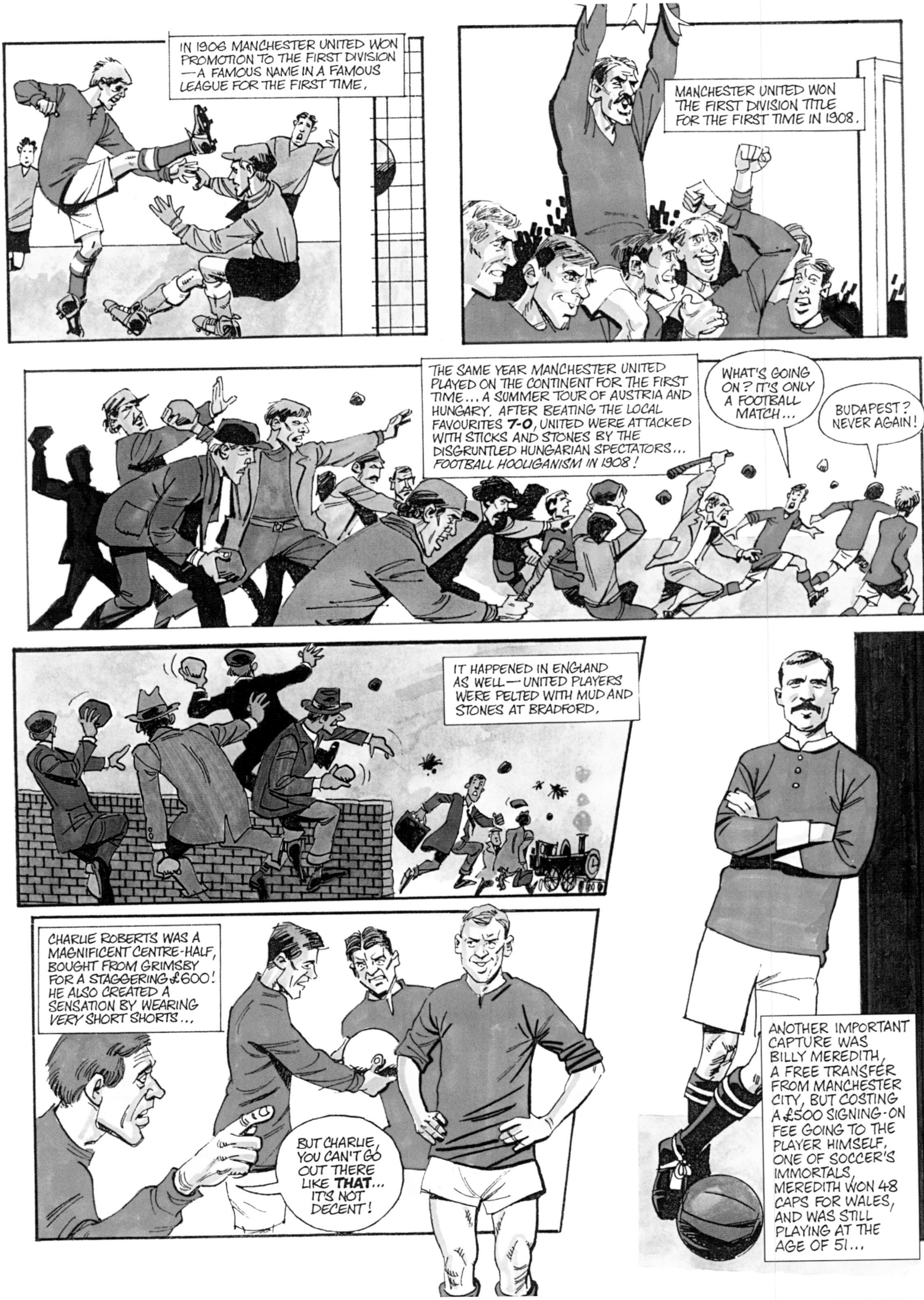
IN 1906 MANCHESTER UNITED WON PROMOTION TO THE FIRST DIVISION —A FAMOUS NAME IN A FAMOUS LEAGUE FOR THE FIRST TIME,
MANCHESTER UNITED WON THE FIRST DIVISION TITLE FOR THE FIRST TIME IN 1908.
THE SAME YEAR MANCHESTER UNITED PLAYED ON THE CONTINENT FOR THE FIRST TIME... A SUMMER TOUR OF AUSTRIA AND HUNGARY. AFTER BEATING THE LOCAL FAVOURITES 7-0, UNITED WERE ATTACKED WITH STICKS AND STONES BY THE DISGRUNTLED HUNGARIAN SPECTATORS... FOOTBALL HOOLIGANISM IN 1908!
WHAT'S GOING ON? IT'S ONLY A FOOTBALL MATCH...
BUDAPEST? NEVER AGAIN!
IT HAPPENED IN ENGLAND AS WELL—UNITED PLAYERS WERE PELTED WITH MUD AND STONES AT BRADFORD.
CHARLIE ROBERTS WAS A MAGNIFICENT CENTRE-HALF, BOUGHT FROM GRIMSBY FOR A STAGGERING £600! HE ALSO CREATED A SENSATION BY WEARING VERY SHORT SHORTS...
BUT CHARLIE, YOU CAN'T GO OUT THERE LIKE THAT... IT'S NOT DECENT!
ANOTHER IMPORTANT CAPTURE WAS BILLY MEREDITH, A FREE TRANSFER FROM MANCHESTER CITY, BUT COSTING A £500 SIGNING-ON FEE GOING TO THE PLAYER HIMSELF, ONE OF SOCCER'S IMMORTALS, MEREDITH WON 48 CAPS FOR WALES, AND WAS STILL PLAYING AT THE AGE OF 51...

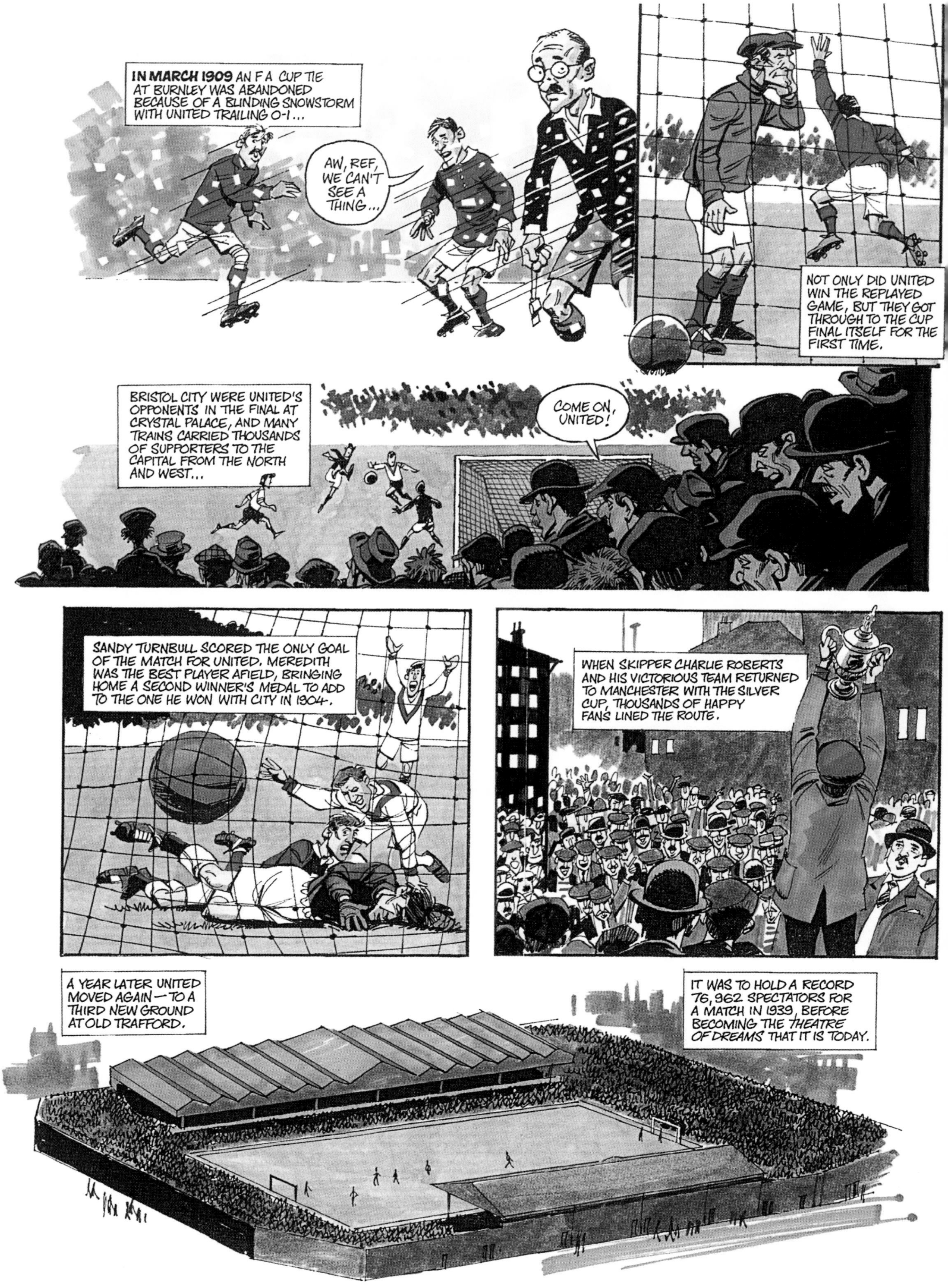
IN MARCH 1909 AN F A CUP TIE AT BURNLEY WAS ABANDONED BECAUSE OF A BLINDING SNOWSTORM WITH UNITED TRAILING 0-1...
AW, REF, WE CAN'T SEE A THING...
NOT ONLY DID UNITED WIN THE REPLAYED GAME, BUT THEY GOT THROUGH TO THE CUP FINAL ITSELF FOR THE FIRST TIME.
BRISTOL CITY WERE UNITED'S OPPONENTS IN THE FINAL AT CRYSTAL PALACE, AND MANY TRAINS CARRIED THOUSANDS OF SUPPORTERS TO THE CAPITAL FROM THE NORTH AND WEST...
COME ON, UNITED!
SANDY TURNBULL SCORED THE ONLY GOAL OF THE MATCH FOR UNITED. MEREDITH WAS THE BEST PLAYER AFIELD, BRINGING HOME A SECOND WINNER'S MEDAL TO ADD TO THE ONE HE WON WITH CITY IN 1904.
WHEN SKIPPER CHARLIE ROBERTS AND HIS VICTORIOUS TEAM RETURNED TO MANCHESTER WITH THE SILVER CUP, THOUSANDS OF HAPPY FANS LINED THE ROUTE.
A YEAR LATER UNITED MOVED AGAIN — TO A THIRD NEW GROUND AT OLD TRAFFORD.
IT WAS TO HOLD A RECORD 76,962 SPECTATORS FOR A MATCH IN 1939, BEFORE BECOMING THE THEATRE OF DREAMS THAT IT IS TODAY.

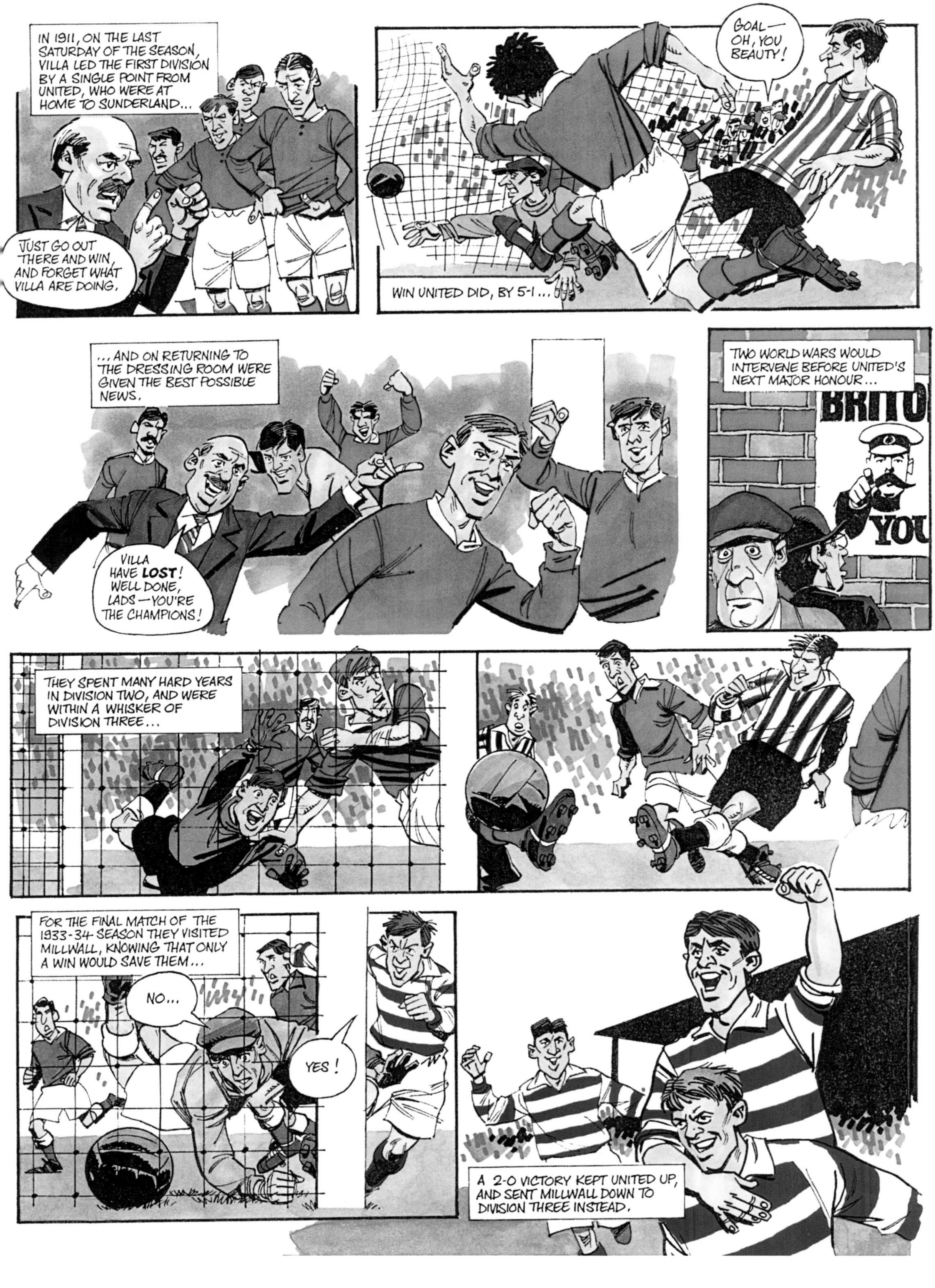
IN 1911, ON THE LAST SATURDAY OF THE SEASON, VILLA LED THE FIRST DIVISION BY A SINGLE POINT FROM UNITED, WHO WERE AT HOME TO SUNDERLAND...
JUST GO OUT THERE AND WIN, AND FORGET WHAT VILLA ARE DOING.
GOAL— OH, YOU BEAUTY!
WIN UNITED DID, BY 5-1...
...AND ON RETURNING TO THE DRESSING ROOM WERE GIVEN THE BEST POSSIBLE NEWS.
VILLA HAVE **LOST**! WELL DONE, LADS—YOU'RE THE CHAMPIONS!
TWO WORLD WARS WOULD INTERVENE BEFORE UNITED'S NEXT MAJOR HONOUR...
THEY SPENT MANY HARD YEARS IN DIVISION TWO, AND WERE WITHIN A WHISKER OF DIVISION THREE...
FOR THE FINAL MATCH OF THE 1933-34 SEASON THEY VISITED MILLWALL, KNOWING THAT ONLY A WIN WOULD SAVE THEM...
NO...
YES!
A 2-0 VICTORY KEPT UNITED UP, AND SENT MILLWALL DOWN TO DIVISION THREE INSTEAD.

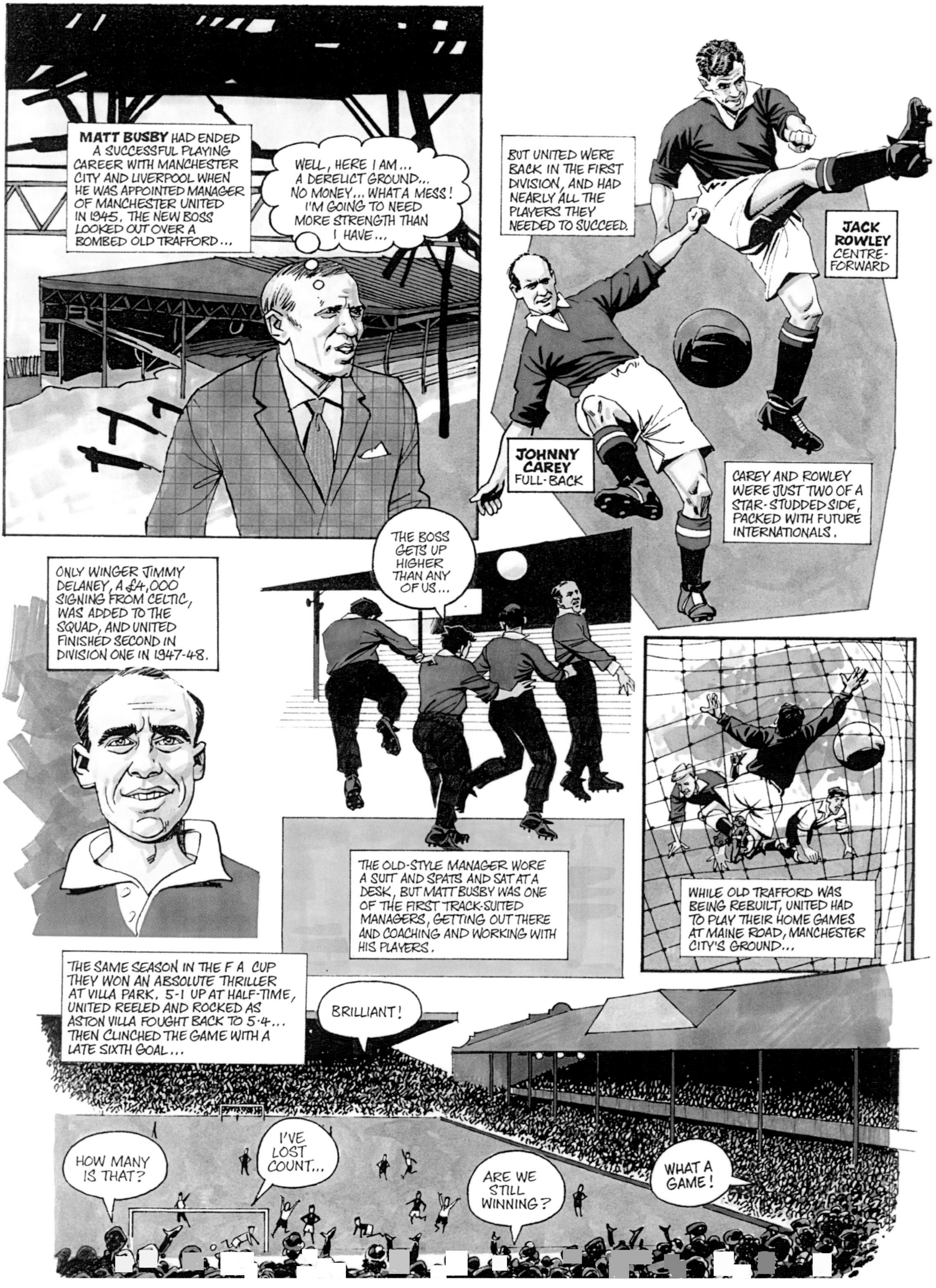
MATT BUSBY HAD ENDED A SUCCESSFUL PLAYING CAREER WITH MANCHESTER CITY AND LIVERPOOL WHEN HE WAS APPOINTED MANAGER OF MANCHESTER UNITED IN 1945. THE NEW BOSS LOOKED OUT OVER A BOMBED OLD TRAFFORD...
WELL, HERE I AM... A DERELICT GROUND... NO MONEY... WHAT A MESS! I'M GOING TO NEED MORE STRENGTH THAN I HAVE...
BUT UNITED WERE BACK IN THE FIRST DIVISION, AND HAD NEARLY ALL THE PLAYERS THEY NEEDED TO SUCCEED.
JACK ROWLEY CENTRE-FORWARD
JOHNNY CAREY FULL-BACK
CAREY AND ROWLEY WERE JUST TWO OF A STAR-STUDDED SIDE, PACKED WITH FUTURE INTERNATIONALS.
ONLY WINGER JIMMY DELANEY, A £4,000 SIGNING FROM CELTIC, WAS ADDED TO THE SQUAD, AND UNITED FINISHED SECOND IN DIVISION ONE IN 1947-48.
THE BOSS GETS UP HIGHER THAN ANY OF US...
THE OLD-STYLE MANAGER WORE A SUIT AND SPATS AND SAT AT A DESK, BUT MATT BUSBY WAS ONE OF THE FIRST TRACK-SUITED MANAGERS, GETTING OUT THERE AND COACHING AND WORKING WITH HIS PLAYERS.
WHILE OLD TRAFFORD WAS BEING REBUILT, UNITED HAD TO PLAY THEIR HOME GAMES AT MAINE ROAD, MANCHESTER CITY'S GROUND...
THE SAME SEASON IN THE F A CUP THEY WON AN ABSOLUTE THRILLER AT VILLA PARK. 5-1 UP AT HALF-TIME, UNITED REELED AND ROCKED AS ASTON VILLA FOUGHT BACK TO 5-4... THEN CLINCHED THE GAME WITH A LATE SIXTH GOAL...
BRILLIANT!
HOW MANY IS THAT?
I'VE LOST COUNT...
ARE WE STILL WINNING?
WHAT A GAME!

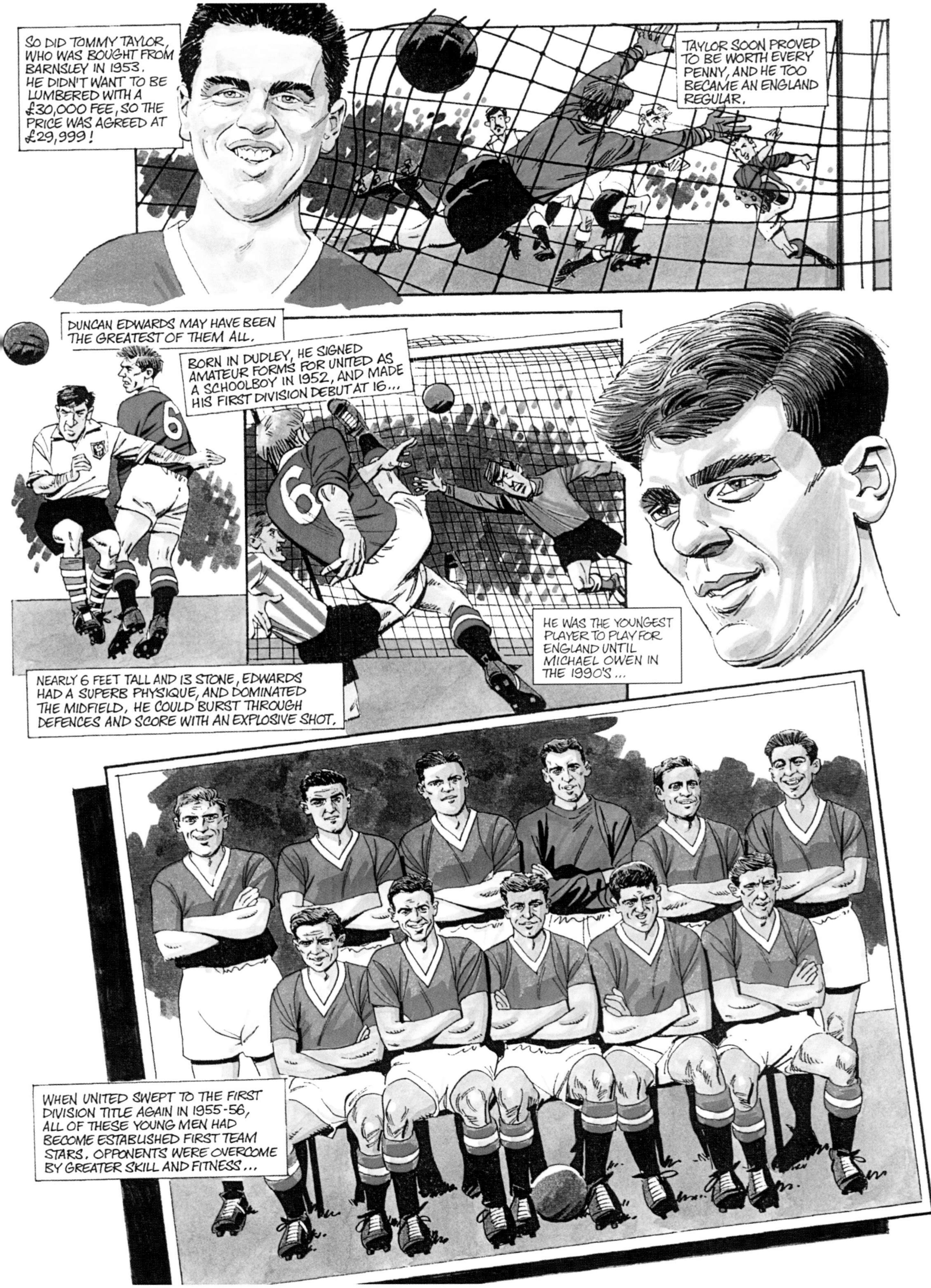
SO DID TOMMY TAYLOR, WHO WAS BOUGHT FROM BARNSLEY IN 1953. HE DIDN'T WANT TO BE LUMBERED WITH A £30,000 FEE, SO THE PRICE WAS AGREED AT £29,999!
TAYLOR SOON PROVED TO BE WORTH EVERY PENNY, AND HE TOO BECAME AN ENGLAND REGULAR.
DUNCAN EDWARDS MAY HAVE BEEN THE GREATEST OF THEM ALL.
BORN IN DUDLEY, HE SIGNED AMATEUR FORMS FOR UNITED AS A SCHOOLBOY IN 1952, AND MADE HIS FIRST DIVISION DEBUT AT 16...
NEARLY 6 FEET TALL AND 13 STONE, EDWARDS HAD A SUPERB PHYSIQUE, AND DOMINATED THE MIDFIELD. HE COULD BURST THROUGH DEFENCES AND SCORE WITH AN EXPLOSIVE SHOT.
HE WAS THE YOUNGEST PLAYER TO PLAY FOR ENGLAND UNTIL MICHAEL OWEN IN THE 1990'S...
WHEN UNITED SWEPT TO THE FIRST DIVISION TITLE AGAIN IN 1955-56, ALL OF THESE YOUNG MEN HAD BECOME ESTABLISHED FIRST TEAM STARS. OPPONENTS WERE OVERCOME BY GREATER SKILL AND FITNESS...

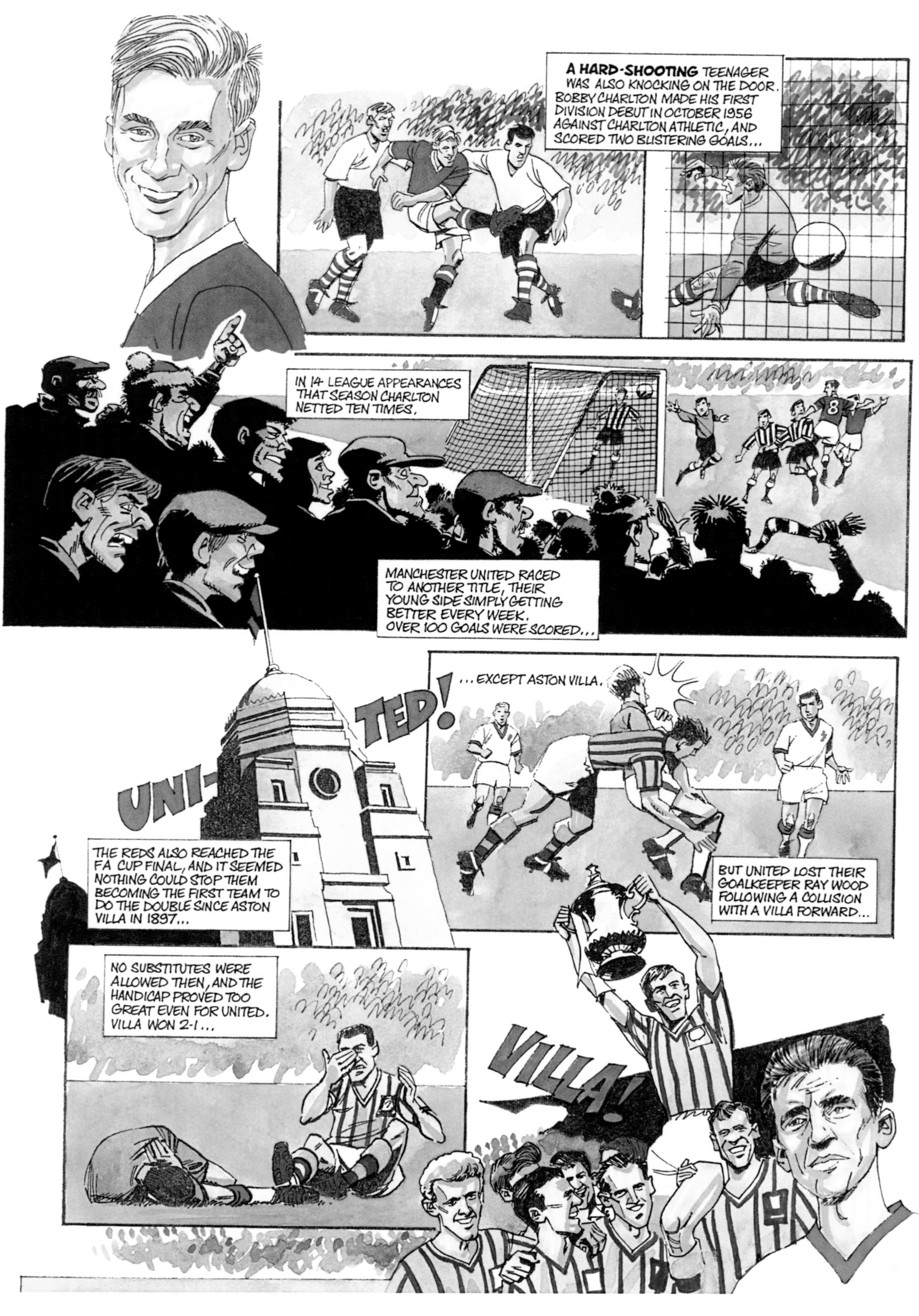
A HARD-SHOOTING TEENAGER WAS ALSO KNOCKING ON THE DOOR. BOBBY CHARLTON MADE HIS FIRST DIVISION DEBUT IN OCTOBER 1956 AGAINST CHARLTON ATHLETIC, AND SCORED TWO BLISTERING GOALS...
IN 14 LEAGUE APPEARANCES THAT SEASON CHARLTON NETTED TEN TIMES.
MANCHESTER UNITED RACED TO ANOTHER TITLE, THEIR YOUNG SIDE SIMPLY GETTING BETTER EVERY WEEK. OVER 100 GOALS WERE SCORED...
UNI-
TED!
THE REDS ALSO REACHED THE FA CUP FINAL, AND IT SEEMED NOTHING COULD STOP THEM BECOMING THE FIRST TEAM TO DO THE DOUBLE SINCE ASTON VILLA IN 1897...
...EXCEPT ASTON VILLA.
BUT UNITED LOST THEIR GOALKEEPER RAY WOOD FOLLOWING A COLLISION WITH A VILLA FORWARD...
NO SUBSTITUTES WERE ALLOWED THEN, AND THE HANDICAP PROVED TOO GREAT EVEN FOR UNITED. VILLA WON 2-1...
VILLA!

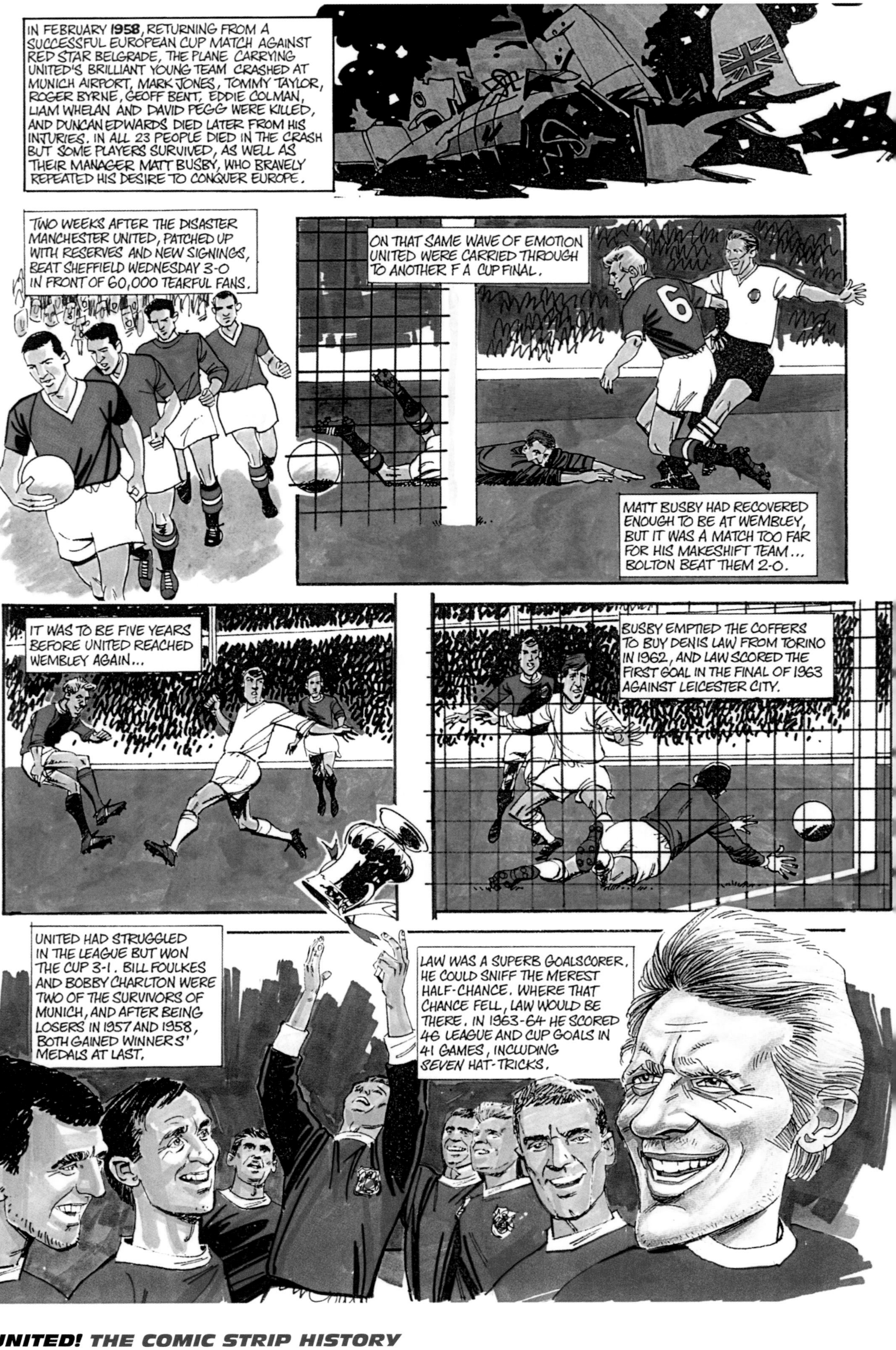
IN FEBRUARY 1958, RETURNING FROM A SUCCESSFUL EUROPEAN CUP MATCH AGAINST RED STAR BELGRADE, THE PLANE CARRYING UNITED'S BRILLIANT YOUNG TEAM CRASHED AT MUNICH AIRPORT. MARK JONES, TOMMY TAYLOR, ROGER BYRNE, GEOFF BENT, EDDIE COLMAN, LIAM WHELAN AND DAVID PEGG WERE KILLED, AND DUNCAN EDWARDS DIED LATER FROM HIS INJURIES. IN ALL 23 PEOPLE DIED IN THE CRASH BUT SOME PLAYERS SURVIVED, AS WELL AS THEIR MANAGER MATT BUSBY, WHO BRAVELY REPEATED HIS DESIRE TO CONQUER EUROPE.
TWO WEEKS AFTER THE DISASTER MANCHESTER UNITED, PATCHED UP WITH RESERVES AND NEW SIGNINGS, BEAT SHEFFIELD WEDNESDAY 3-0 IN FRONT OF 60,000 TEARFUL FANS.
ON THAT SAME WAVE OF EMOTION UNITED WERE CARRIED THROUGH TO ANOTHER F A CUP FINAL.
6
MATT BUSBY HAD RECOVERED ENOUGH TO BE AT WEMBLEY, BUT IT WAS A MATCH TOO FAR FOR HIS MAKESHIFT TEAM... BOLTON BEAT THEM 2-0.
IT WAS TO BE FIVE YEARS BEFORE UNITED REACHED WEMBLEY AGAIN...
BUSBY EMPTIED THE COFFERS TO BUY DENIS LAW FROM TORINO IN 1962, AND LAW SCORED THE FIRST GOAL IN THE FINAL OF 1963 AGAINST LEICESTER CITY.
UNITED HAD STRUGGLED IN THE LEAGUE BUT WON THE CUP 3-1. BILL FOULKES AND BOBBY CHARLTON WERE TWO OF THE SURVIVORS OF MUNICH, AND AFTER BEING LOSERS IN 1957 AND 1958, BOTH GAINED WINNERS' MEDALS AT LAST.
LAW WAS A SUPERB GOALSCORER. HE COULD SNIFF THE MEREST HALF-CHANCE. WHERE THAT CHANCE FELL, LAW WOULD BE THERE. IN 1963-64 HE SCORED 46 LEAGUE AND CUP GOALS IN 41 GAMES, INCLUDING SEVEN HAT-TRICKS.

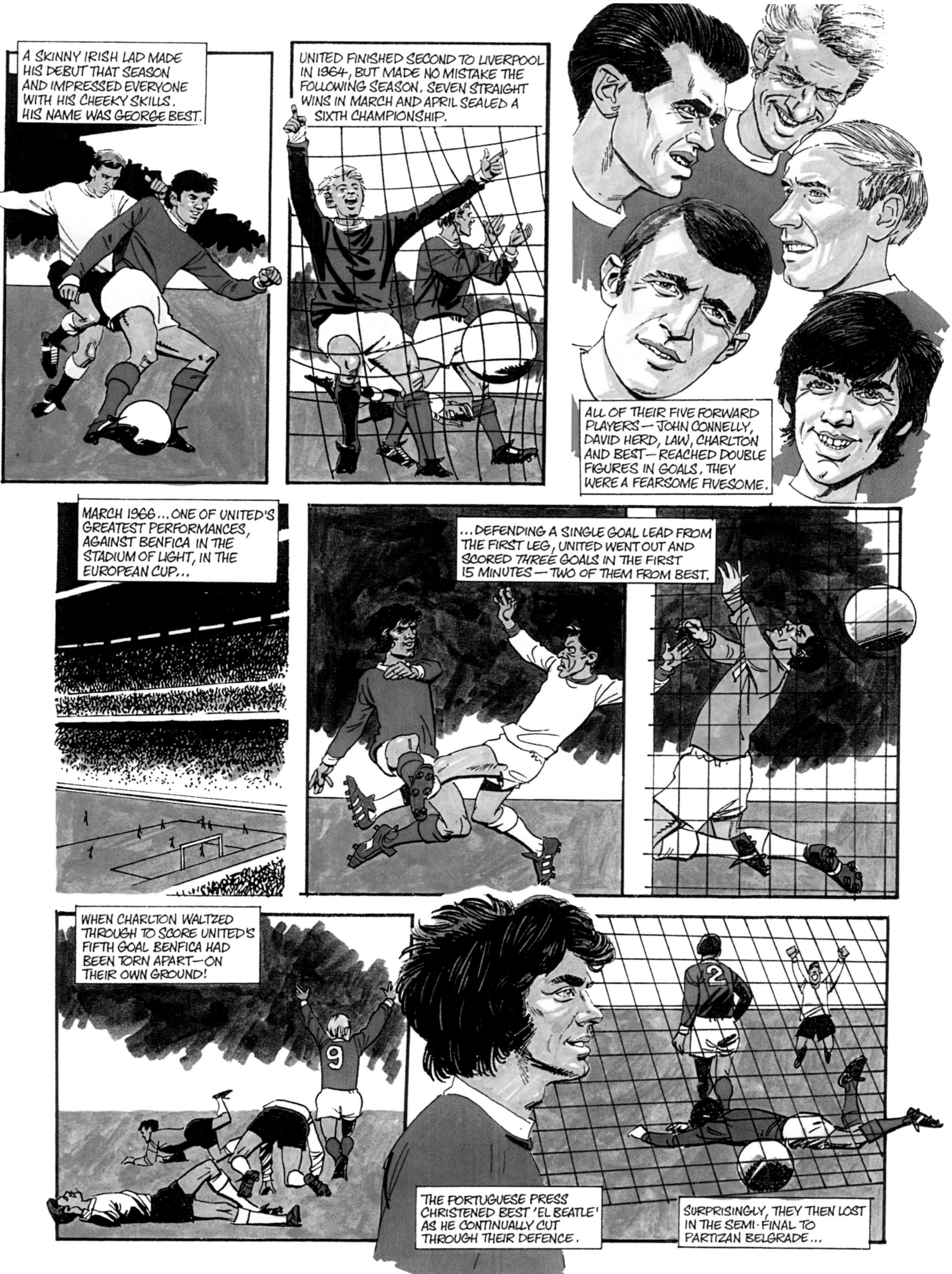
A SKINNY IRISH LAD MADE HIS DEBUT THAT SEASON AND IMPRESSED EVERYONE WITH HIS CHEEKY SKILLS. HIS NAME WAS GEORGE BEST.
UNITED FINISHED SECOND TO LIVERPOOL IN 1964, BUT MADE NO MISTAKE THE FOLLOWING SEASON. SEVEN STRAIGHT WINS IN MARCH AND APRIL SEALED A SIXTH CHAMPIONSHIP.
ALL OF THEIR FIVE FORWARD PLAYERS — JOHN CONNELLY, DAVID HERD, LAW, CHARLTON AND BEST — REACHED DOUBLE FIGURES IN GOALS. THEY WERE A FEARSOME FIVESOME.
MARCH 1966... ONE OF UNITED'S GREATEST PERFORMANCES, AGAINST BENFICA IN THE STADIUM OF LIGHT, IN THE EUROPEAN CUP...
...DEFENDING A SINGLE GOAL LEAD FROM THE FIRST LEG, UNITED WENT OUT AND SCORED THREE GOALS IN THE FIRST 15 MINUTES — TWO OF THEM FROM BEST.
WHEN CHARLTON WALTZED THROUGH TO SCORE UNITED'S FIFTH GOAL BENFICA HAD BEEN TORN APART — ON THEIR OWN GROUND!
9
2
THE PORTUGUESE PRESS CHRISTENED BEST 'EL BEATLE' AS HE CONTINUALLY CUT THROUGH THEIR DEFENCE.
SURPRISINGLY, THEY THEN LOST IN THE SEMI-FINAL TO PARTIZAN BELGRADE...

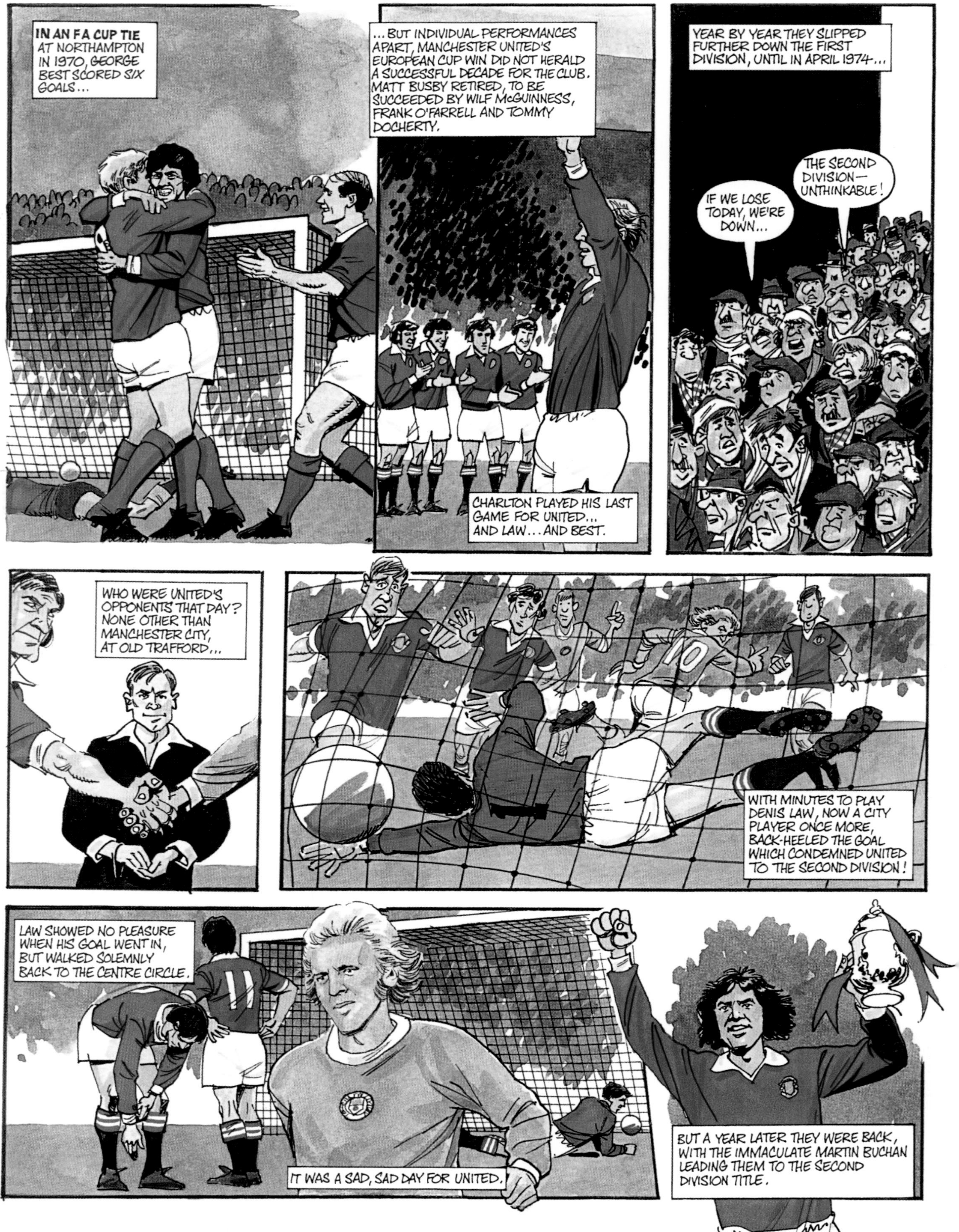
IN AN F A CUP TIE AT NORTHAMPTON IN 1970, GEORGE BEST SCORED SIX GOALS...
...BUT INDIVIDUAL PERFORMANCES APART, MANCHESTER UNITED'S EUROPEAN CUP WIN DID NOT HERALD A SUCCESSFUL DECADE FOR THE CLUB. MATT BUSBY RETIRED, TO BE SUCCEEDED BY WILF McGUINNESS, FRANK O'FARRELL AND TOMMY DOCHERTY.
CHARLTON PLAYED HIS LAST GAME FOR UNITED... AND LAW... AND BEST.
YEAR BY YEAR THEY SLIPPED FURTHER DOWN THE FIRST DIVISION, UNTIL IN APRIL 1974...
IF WE LOSE TODAY, WE'RE DOWN...
THE SECOND DIVISION— UNTHINKABLE!
WHO WERE UNITED'S OPPONENTS THAT DAY? NONE OTHER THAN MANCHESTER CITY, AT OLD TRAFFORD...
WITH MINUTES TO PLAY DENIS LAW, NOW A CITY PLAYER ONCE MORE, BACK-HEELED THE GOAL WHICH CONDEMNED UNITED TO THE SECOND DIVISION!
LAW SHOWED NO PLEASURE WHEN HIS GOAL WENT IN, BUT WALKED SOLEMNLY BACK TO THE CENTRE CIRCLE.
IT WAS A SAD, SAD DAY FOR UNITED.
BUT A YEAR LATER THEY WERE BACK, WITH THE IMMACULATE MARTIN BUCHAN LEADING THEM TO THE SECOND DIVISION TITLE.

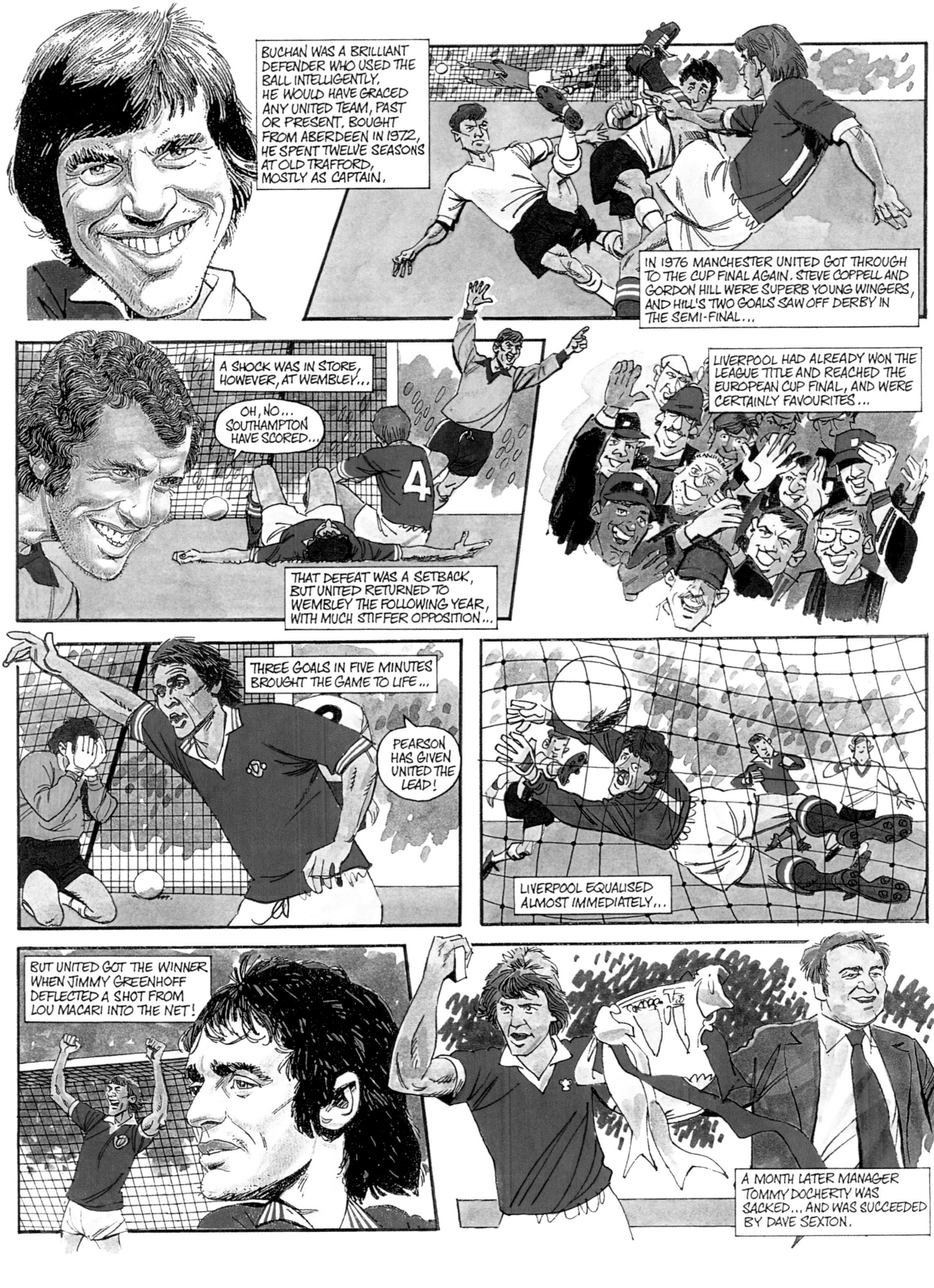
BUCHAN WAS A BRILLIANT DEFENDER WHO USED THE BALL INTELLIGENTLY. HE WOULD HAVE GRACED ANY UNITED TEAM, PAST OR PRESENT. BOUGHT FROM ABERDEEN IN 1972, HE SPENT TWELVE SEASONS AT OLD TRAFFORD, MOSTLY AS CAPTAIN.
IN 1976 MANCHESTER UNITED GOT THROUGH TO THE CUP FINAL AGAIN. STEVE COPPELL AND GORDON HILL WERE SUPERB YOUNG WINGERS, AND HILL'S TWO GOALS SAW OFF DERBY IN THE SEMI-FINAL...
A SHOCK WAS IN STORE, HOWEVER, AT WEMBLEY...
OH, NO... SOUTHAMPTON HAVE SCORED...
4
THAT DEFEAT WAS A SETBACK, BUT UNITED RETURNED TO WEMBLEY THE FOLLOWING YEAR, WITH MUCH STIFFER OPPOSITION...
LIVERPOOL HAD ALREADY WON THE LEAGUE TITLE AND REACHED THE EUROPEAN CUP FINAL, AND WERE CERTAINLY FAVOURITES...
THREE GOALS IN FIVE MINUTES BROUGHT THE GAME TO LIFE...
PEARSON HAS GIVEN UNITED THE LEAD!
LIVERPOOL EQUALISED ALMOST IMMEDIATELY...
BUT UNITED GOT THE WINNER WHEN JIMMY GREENHOFF DEFLECTED A SHOT FROM LOU MACARI INTO THE NET!
A MONTH LATER MANAGER TOMMY DOCHERTY WAS SACKED... AND WAS SUCCEEDED BY DAVE SEXTON.

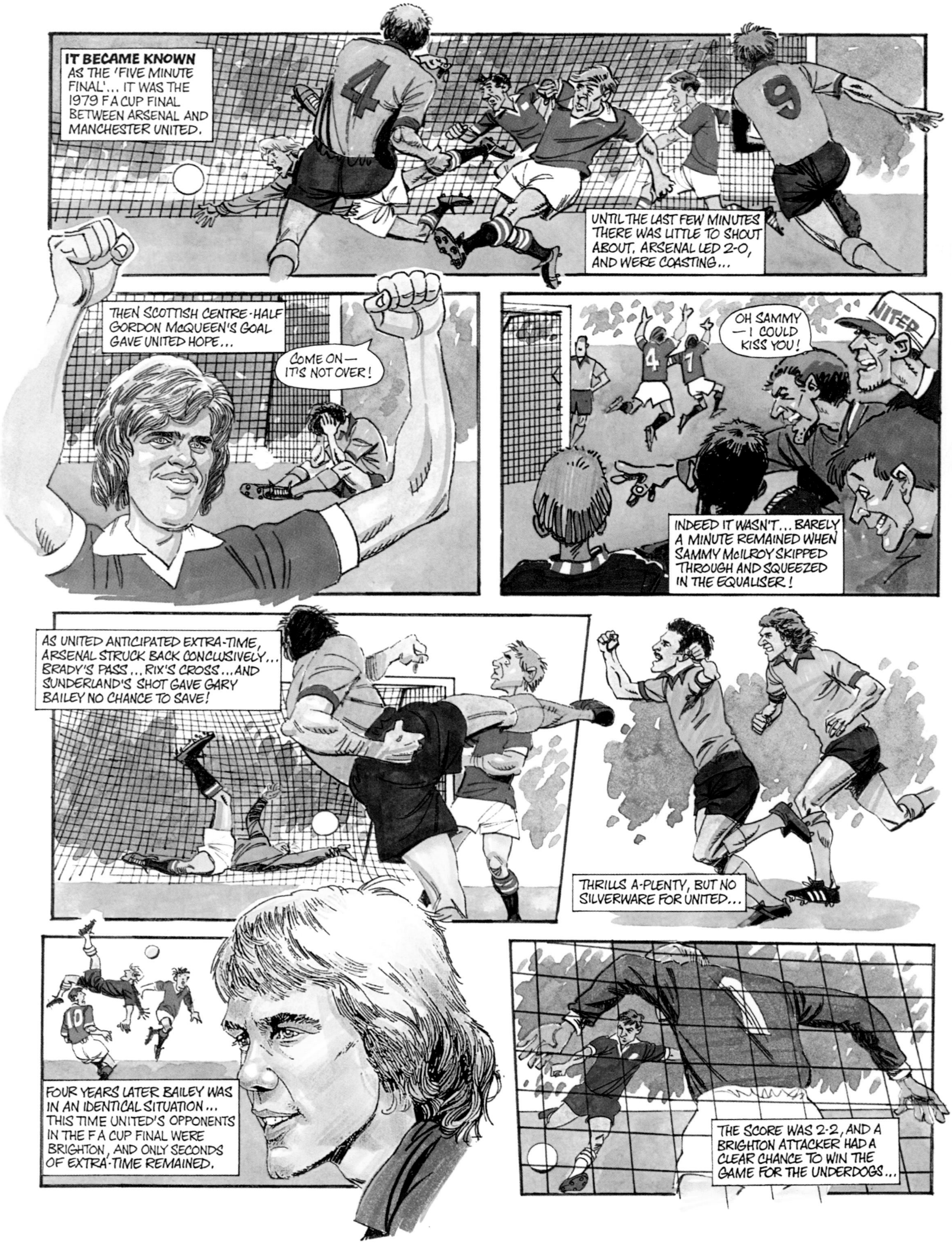
IT BECAME KNOWN AS THE 'FIVE MINUTE FINAL'... IT WAS THE 1979 F A CUP FINAL BETWEEN ARSENAL AND MANCHESTER UNITED.
UNTIL THE LAST FEW MINUTES THERE WAS LITTLE TO SHOUT ABOUT, ARSENAL LED 2-0, AND WERE COASTING...
THEN SCOTTISH CENTRE-HALF GORDON McQUEEN'S GOAL GAVE UNITED HOPE...
COME ON — IT'S NOT OVER!
OH SAMMY — I COULD KISS YOU!
INDEED IT WASN'T... BARELY A MINUTE REMAINED WHEN SAMMY McILROY SKIPPED THROUGH AND SQUEEZED IN THE EQUALISER!
AS UNITED ANTICIPATED EXTRA-TIME, ARSENAL STRUCK BACK CONCLUSIVELY... BRADY'S PASS... RIX'S CROSS... AND SUNDERLAND'S SHOT GAVE GARY BAILEY NO CHANCE TO SAVE!
THRILLS A-PLENTY, BUT NO SILVERWARE FOR UNITED...
FOUR YEARS LATER BAILEY WAS IN AN IDENTICAL SITUATION... THIS TIME UNITED'S OPPONENTS IN THE F A CUP FINAL WERE BRIGHTON, AND ONLY SECONDS OF EXTRA-TIME REMAINED.
THE SCORE WAS 2-2, AND A BRIGHTON ATTACKER HAD A CLEAR CHANCE TO WIN THE GAME FOR THE UNDERDOGS...

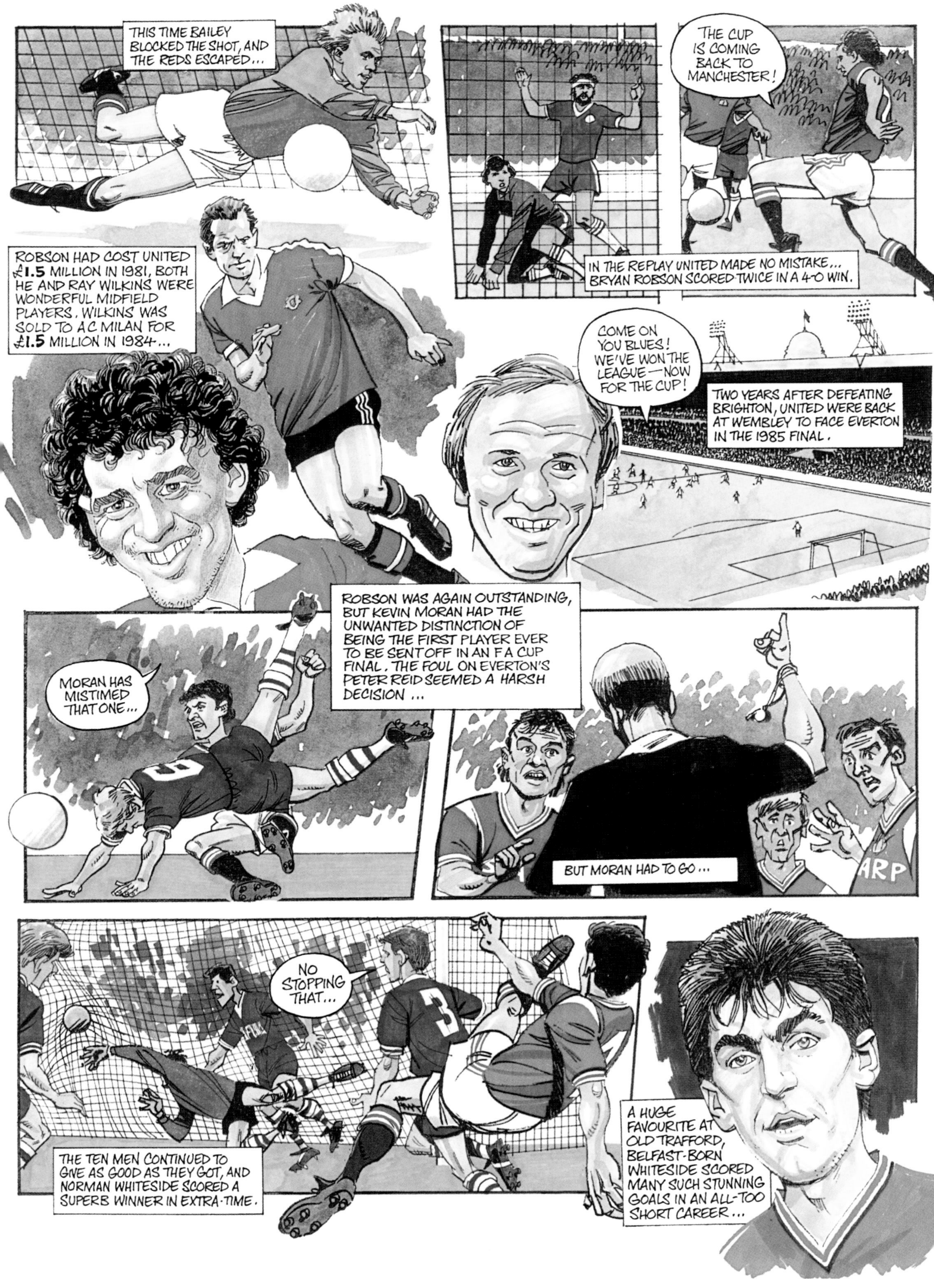
THIS TIME BAILEY BLOCKED THE SHOT, AND THE REDS ESCAPED...
THE CUP IS COMING BACK TO MANCHESTER!
IN THE REPLAY UNITED MADE NO MISTAKE... BRYAN ROBSON SCORED TWICE IN A 4-0 WIN.
ROBSON HAD COST UNITED £1.5 MILLION IN 1981, BOTH HE AND RAY WILKINS WERE WONDERFUL MIDFIELD PLAYERS. WILKINS WAS SOLD TO A C MILAN FOR £1.5 MILLION IN 1984...
COME ON YOU BLUES! WE'VE WON THE LEAGUE — NOW FOR THE CUP!
TWO YEARS AFTER DEFEATING BRIGHTON, UNITED WERE BACK AT WEMBLEY TO FACE EVERTON IN THE 1985 FINAL.
ROBSON WAS AGAIN OUTSTANDING, BUT KEVIN MORAN HAD THE UNWANTED DISTINCTION OF BEING THE FIRST PLAYER EVER TO BE SENT OFF IN AN FA CUP FINAL. THE FOUL ON EVERTON'S PETER REID SEEMED A HARSH DECISION ...
MORAN HAS MISTIMED THAT ONE...
BUT MORAN HAD TO GO...
NO STOPPING THAT...
THE TEN MEN CONTINUED TO GIVE AS GOOD AS THEY GOT, AND NORMAN WHITESIDE SCORED A SUPERB WINNER IN EXTRA-TIME.
A HUGE FAVOURITE AT OLD TRAFFORD, BELFAST-BORN WHITESIDE SCORED MANY SUCH STUNNING GOALS IN AN ALL-TOO SHORT CAREER...

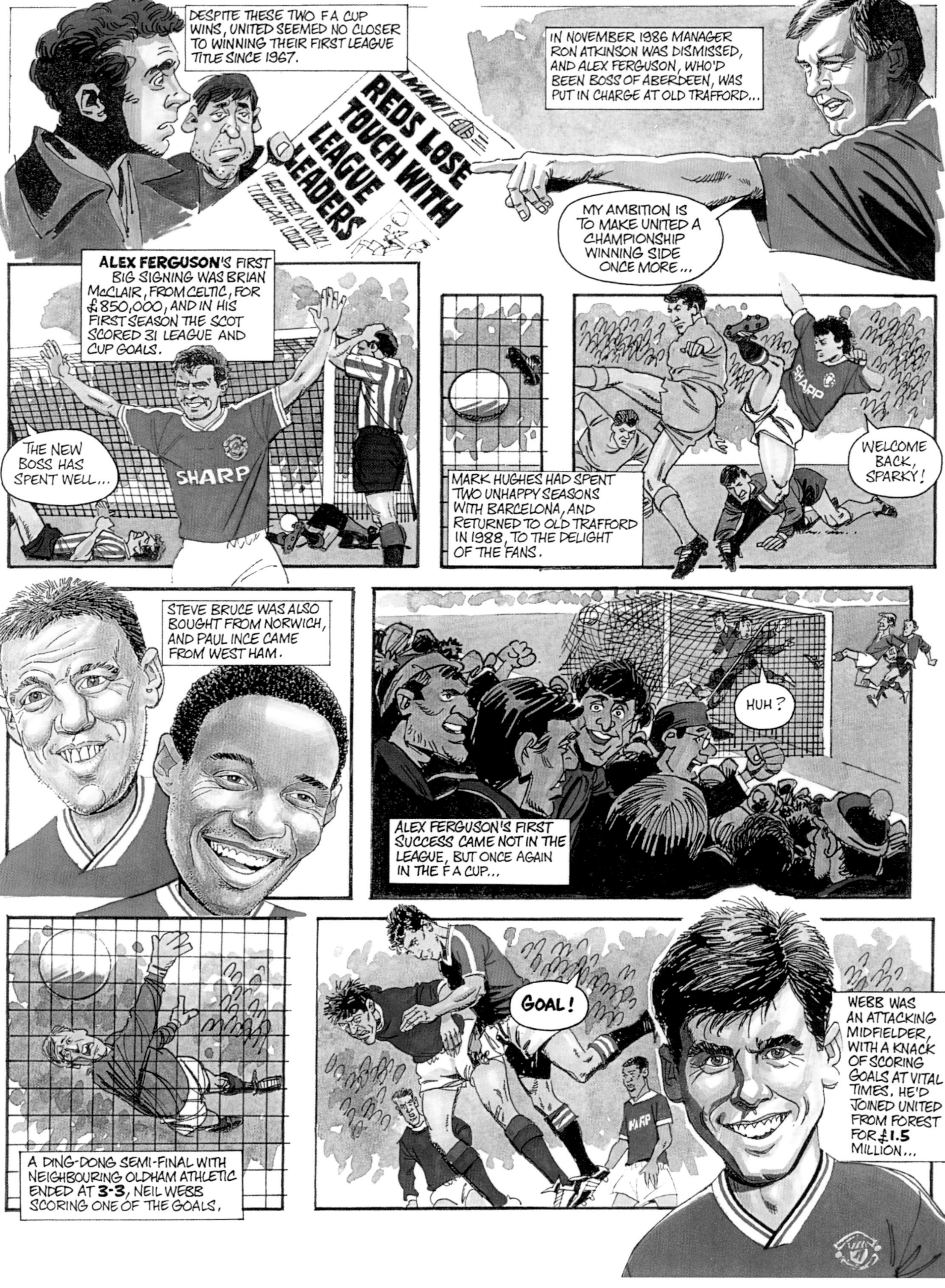
DESPITE THESE TWO F A CUP WINS, UNITED SEEMED NO CLOSER TO WINNING THEIR FIRST LEAGUE TITLE SINCE 1967.
REDS LOSE TOUCH WITH LEAGUE LEADERS
IN NOVEMBER 1986 MANAGER RON ATKINSON WAS DISMISSED, AND ALEX FERGUSON, WHO'D BEEN BOSS OF ABERDEEN, WAS PUT IN CHARGE AT OLD TRAFFORD...
MY AMBITION IS TO MAKE UNITED A CHAMPIONSHIP WINNING SIDE ONCE MORE...
ALEX FERGUSON'S FIRST BIG SIGNING WAS BRIAN McCLAIR, FROM CELTIC, FOR £850,000, AND IN HIS FIRST SEASON THE SCOT SCORED 31 LEAGUE AND CUP GOALS.
THE NEW BOSS HAS SPENT WELL...
SHARP
MARK HUGHES HAD SPENT TWO UNHAPPY SEASONS WITH BARCELONA, AND RETURNED TO OLD TRAFFORD IN 1988, TO THE DELIGHT OF THE FANS.
WELCOME BACK, SPARKY!
STEVE BRUCE WAS ALSO BOUGHT FROM NORWICH, AND PAUL INCE CAME FROM WEST HAM.
HUH?
ALEX FERGUSON'S FIRST SUCCESS CAME NOT IN THE LEAGUE, BUT ONCE AGAIN IN THE F A CUP...
A DING-DONG SEMI-FINAL WITH NEIGHBOURING OLDHAM ATHLETIC ENDED AT 3-3, NEIL WEBB SCORING ONE OF THE GOALS.
GOAL!
WEBB WAS AN ATTACKING MIDFIELDER, WITH A KNACK OF SCORING GOALS AT VITAL TIMES. HE'D JOINED UNITED FROM FOREST FOR £1.5 MILLION...

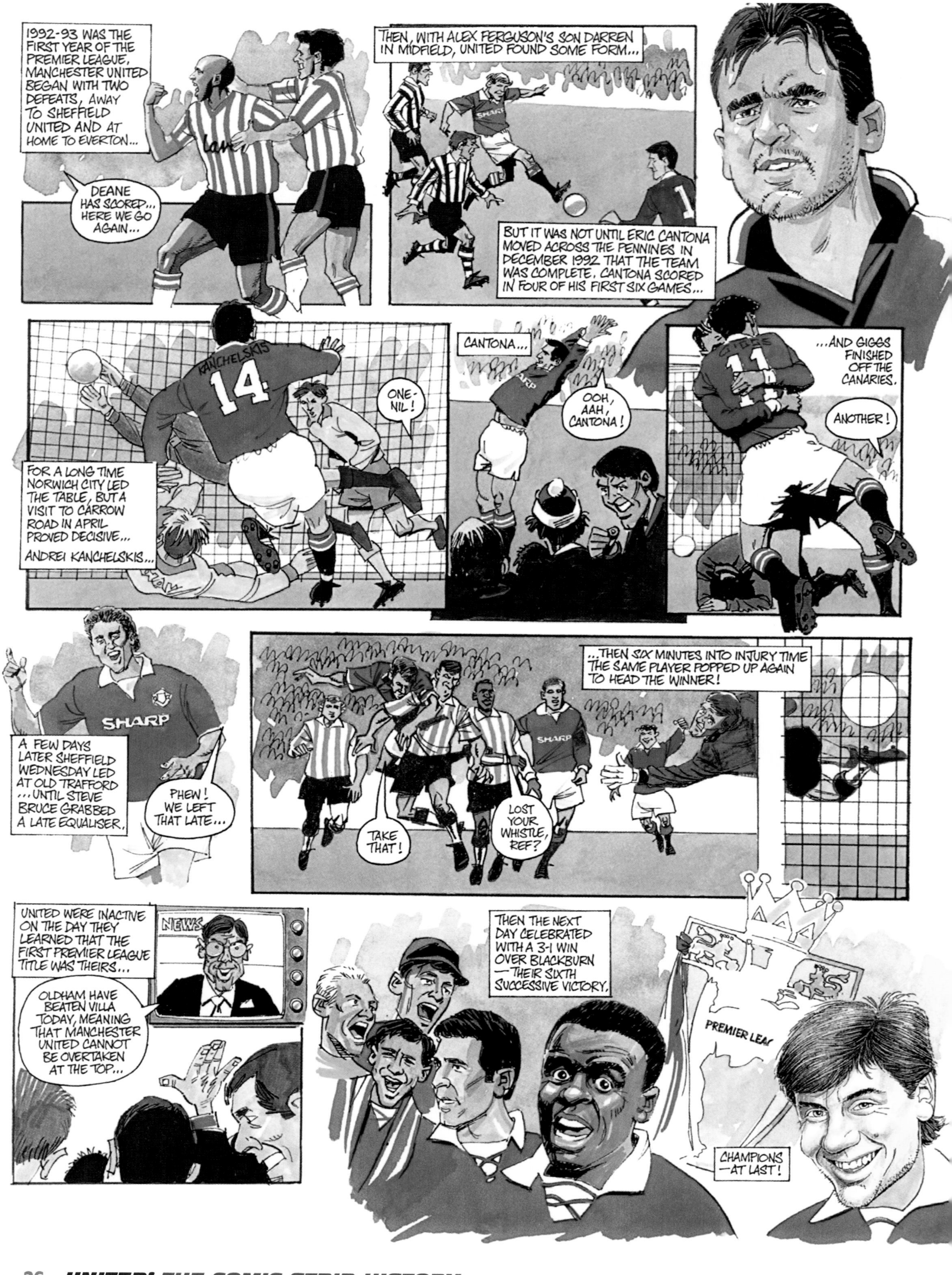
1992-93 WAS THE FIRST YEAR OF THE PREMIER LEAGUE. MANCHESTER UNITED BEGAN WITH TWO DEFEATS, AWAY TO SHEFFIELD UNITED AND AT HOME TO EVERTON...
DEANE HAS SCORED... HERE WE GO AGAIN...
THEN, WITH ALEX FERGUSON'S SON DARREN IN MIDFIELD, UNITED FOUND SOME FORM...
BUT IT WAS NOT UNTIL ERIC CANTONA MOVED ACROSS THE PENNINES IN DECEMBER 1992 THAT THE TEAM WAS COMPLETE. CANTONA SCORED IN FOUR OF HIS FIRST SIX GAMES...
FOR A LONG TIME NORWICH CITY LED THE TABLE, BUT A VISIT TO CARROW ROAD IN APRIL PROVED DECISIVE...
ANDREI KANCHELSKIS...
ONE-NIL!
CANTONA...
OOH, AAH, CANTONA!
...AND GIGGS FINISHED OFF THE CANARIES.
ANOTHER!
A FEW DAYS LATER SHEFFIELD WEDNESDAY LED AT OLD TRAFFORD ...UNTIL STEVE BRUCE GRABBED A LATE EQUALISER.
PHEW! WE LEFT THAT LATE...
...THEN SIX MINUTES INTO INJURY TIME THE SAME PLAYER POPPED UP AGAIN TO HEAD THE WINNER!
TAKE THAT!
LOST YOUR WHISTLE, REF?
UNITED WERE INACTIVE ON THE DAY THEY LEARNED THAT THE FIRST PREMIER LEAGUE TITLE WAS THEIRS...
NEWS
OLDHAM HAVE BEATEN VILLA TODAY, MEANING THAT MANCHESTER UNITED CANNOT BE OVERTAKEN AT THE TOP...
THEN THE NEXT DAY CELEBRATED WITH A 3-1 WIN OVER BLACKBURN —THEIR SIXTH SUCCESSIVE VICTORY.
PREMIER LEA
CHAMPIONS —AT LAST!

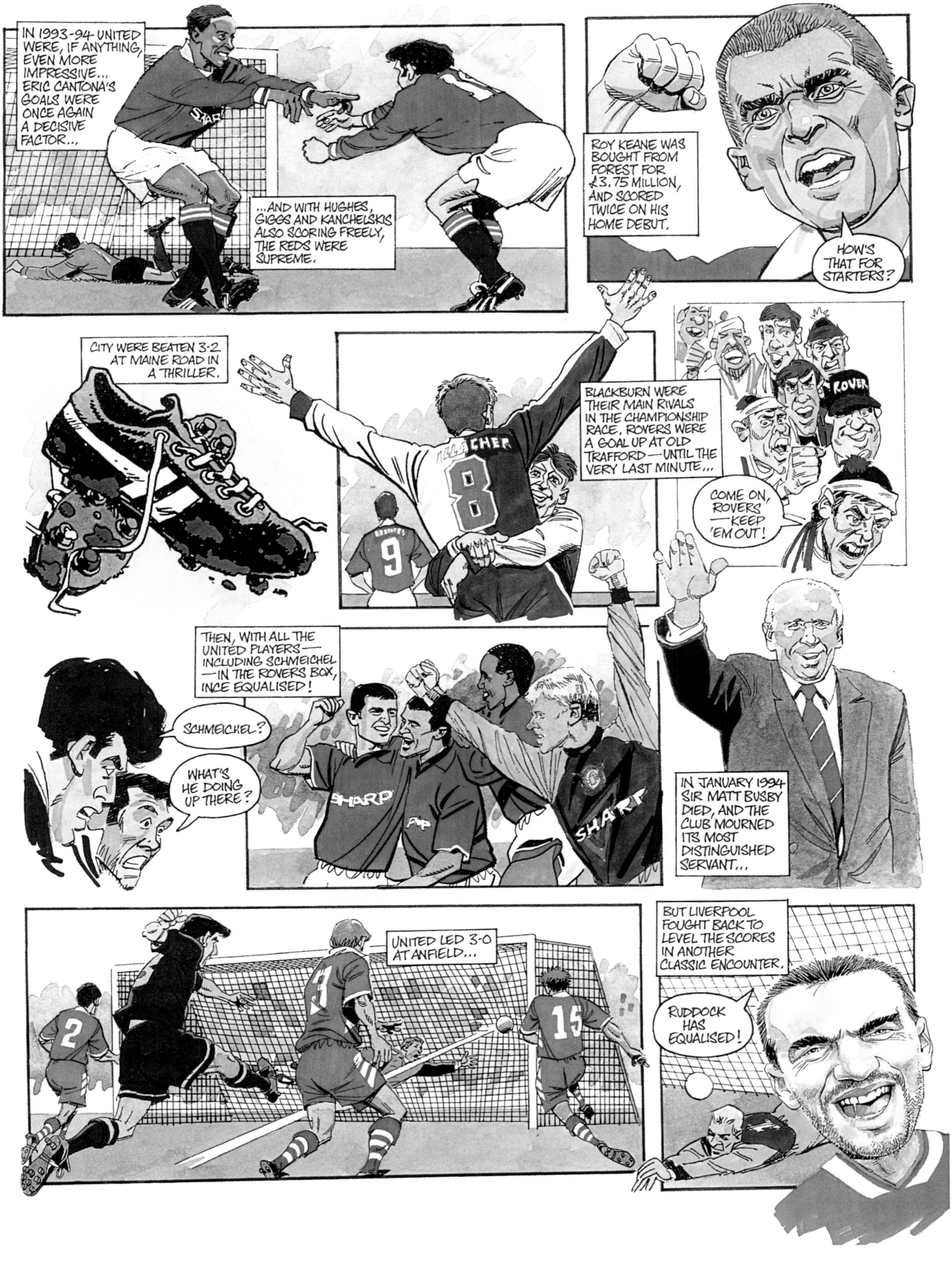

IN 1993-94 UNITED WERE, IF ANYTHING, EVEN MORE IMPRESSIVE... ERIC CANTONA'S GOALS WERE ONCE AGAIN A DECISIVE FACTOR...
...AND WITH HUGHES, GIGGS AND KANCHELSKIS ALSO SCORING FREELY, THE REDS WERE SUPREME.
ROY KEANE WAS BOUGHT FROM FOREST FOR £3.75 MILLION, AND SCORED TWICE ON HIS HOME DEBUT.
HOW'S THAT FOR STARTERS?
CITY WERE BEATEN 3-2 AT MAINE ROAD IN A THRILLER.
BLACKBURN WERE THEIR MAIN RIVALS IN THE CHAMPIONSHIP RACE, ROVERS WERE A GOAL UP AT OLD TRAFFORD — UNTIL THE VERY LAST MINUTE...
COME ON, ROVERS — KEEP 'EM OUT!
THEN, WITH ALL THE UNITED PLAYERS — INCLUDING SCHMEICHEL — IN THE ROVERS BOX, INCE EQUALISED!
SCHMEICHEL?
WHAT'S HE DOING UP THERE?
IN JANUARY 1994 SIR MATT BUSBY DIED, AND THE CLUB MOURNED ITS MOST DISTINGUISHED SERVANT...
UNITED LED 3-0 AT ANFIELD...
BUT LIVERPOOL FOUGHT BACK TO LEVEL THE SCORES IN ANOTHER CLASSIC ENCOUNTER.
RUDDOCK HAS EQUALISED!

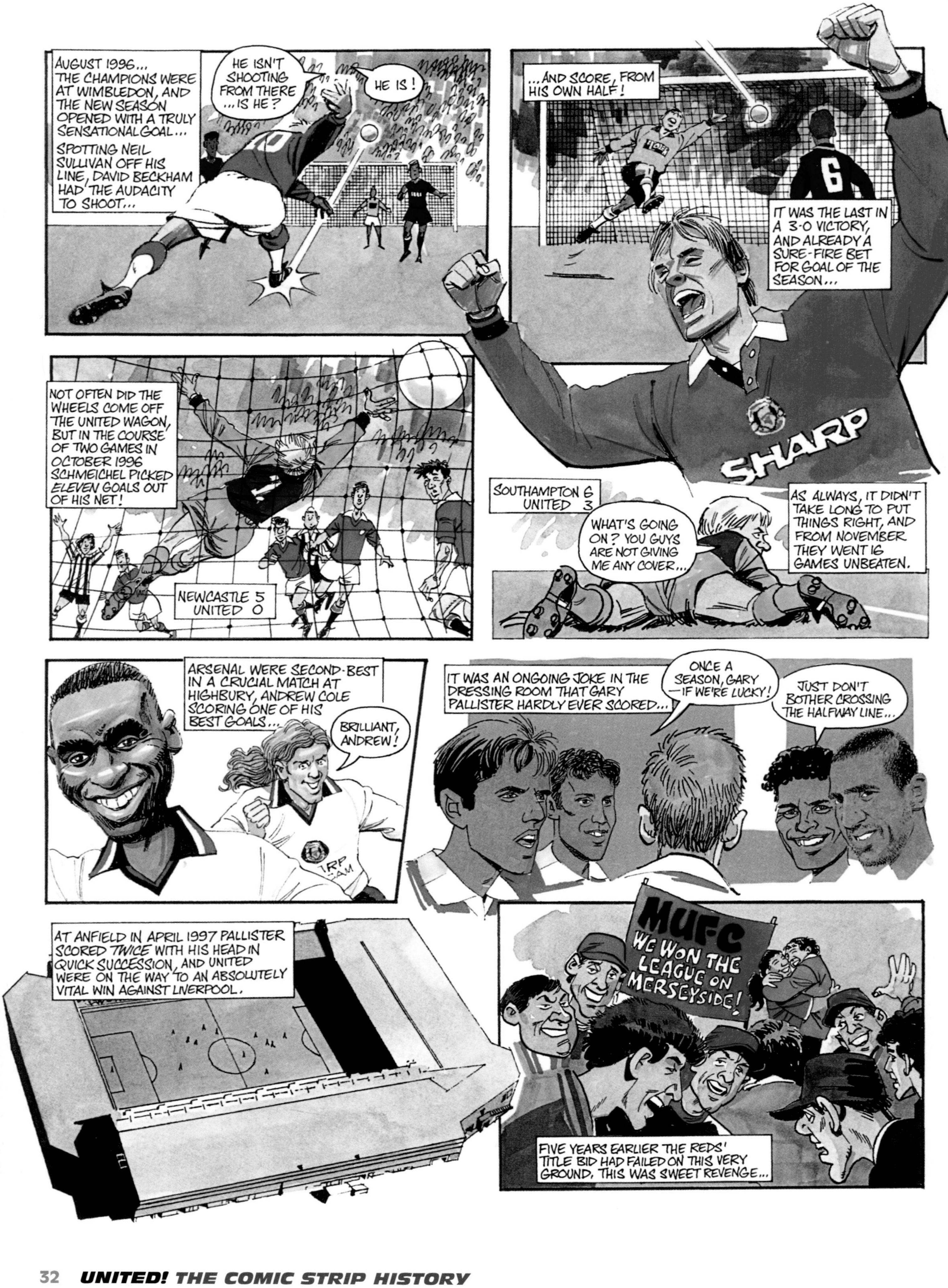

AUGUST 1996... THE CHAMPIONS WERE AT WIMBLEDON, AND THE NEW SEASON OPENED WITH A TRULY SENSATIONAL GOAL...
SPOTTING NEIL SULLIVAN OFF HIS LINE, DAVID BECKHAM HAD THE AUDACITY TO SHOOT...
HE ISN'T SHOOTING FROM THERE ...IS HE?
HE IS!
...AND SCORE, FROM HIS OWN HALF!
IT WAS THE LAST IN A 3-0 VICTORY, AND ALREADY A SURE-FIRE BET FOR GOAL OF THE SEASON...
SHARP
NOT OFTEN DID THE WHEELS COME OFF THE UNITED WAGON, BUT IN THE COURSE OF TWO GAMES IN OCTOBER 1996 SCHMEICHEL PICKED *ELEVEN* GOALS OUT OF HIS NET!
NEWCASTLE 5 UNITED 0
SOUTHAMPTON 6 UNITED 3
WHAT'S GOING ON? YOU GUYS ARE NOT GIVING ME ANY COVER...
AS ALWAYS, IT DIDN'T TAKE LONG TO PUT THINGS RIGHT, AND FROM NOVEMBER THEY WENT 16 GAMES UNBEATEN.
ARSENAL WERE SECOND-BEST IN A CRUCIAL MATCH AT HIGHBURY, ANDREW COLE SCORING ONE OF HIS BEST GOALS...
BRILLIANT, ANDREW!
IT WAS AN ONGOING JOKE IN THE DRESSING ROOM THAT GARY PALLISTER HARDLY EVER SCORED...
ONCE A SEASON, GARY —IF WE'RE LUCKY!
JUST DON'T BOTHER CROSSING THE HALFWAY LINE...
AT ANFIELD IN APRIL 1997 PALLISTER SCORED *TWICE* WITH HIS HEAD IN QUICK SUCCESSION, AND UNITED WERE ON THE WAY TO AN ABSOLUTELY VITAL WIN AGAINST LIVERPOOL.
MUFC WE WON THE LEAGUE ON MERSEYSIDE!
FIVE YEARS EARLIER THE REDS' TITLE BID HAD FAILED ON THIS VERY GROUND, THIS WAS SWEET REVENGE...

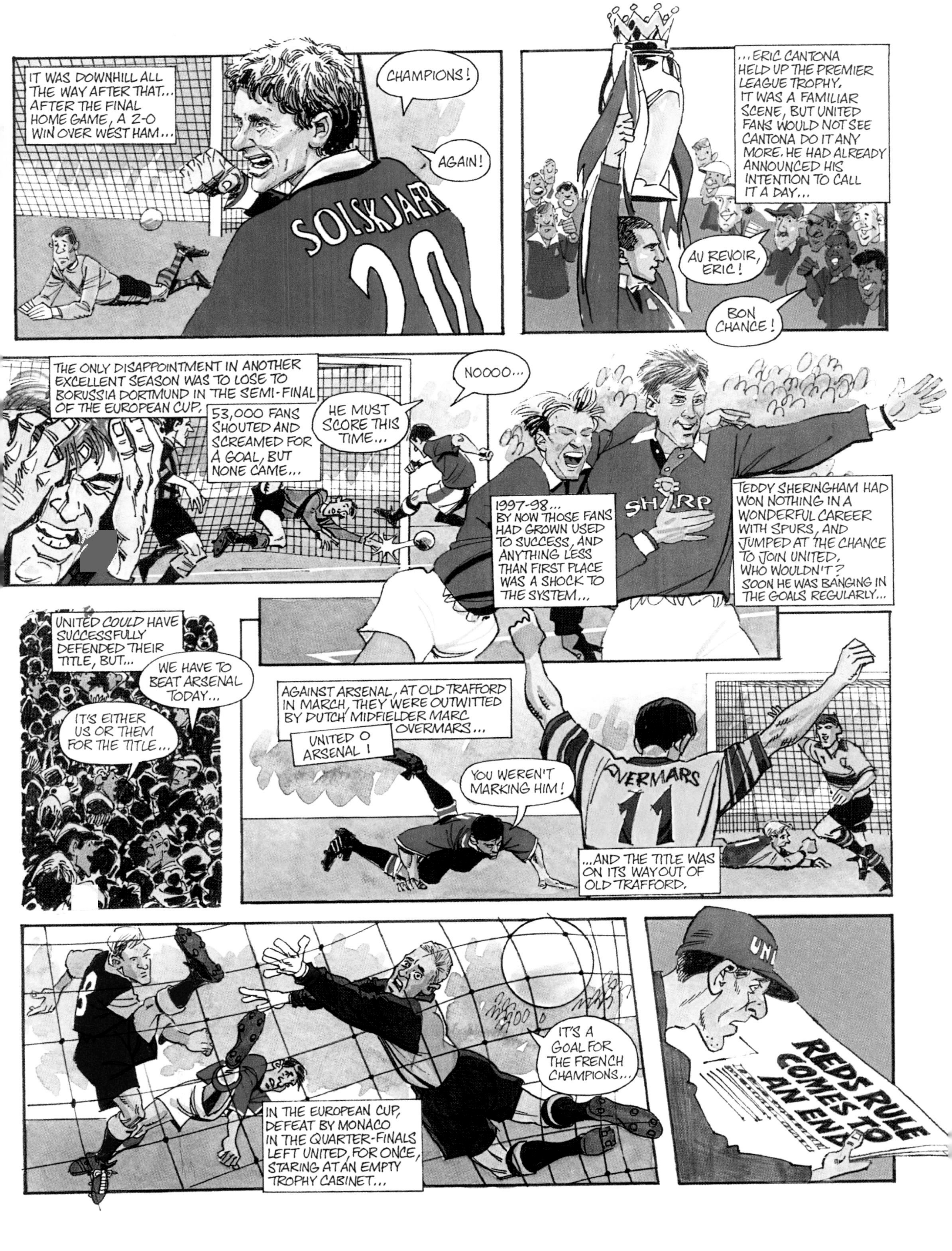
IT WAS DOWNHILL ALL THE WAY AFTER THAT... AFTER THE FINAL HOME GAME, A 2-0 WIN OVER WEST HAM...
CHAMPIONS!
AGAIN!
SOLSKJAER
...ERIC CANTONA HELD UP THE PREMIER LEAGUE TROPHY. IT WAS A FAMILIAR SCENE, BUT UNITED FANS WOULD NOT SEE CANTONA DO IT ANY MORE. HE HAD ALREADY ANNOUNCED HIS INTENTION TO CALL IT A DAY...
AU REVOIR, ERIC!
BON CHANCE!
THE ONLY DISAPPOINTMENT IN ANOTHER EXCELLENT SEASON WAS TO LOSE TO BORUSSIA DORTMUND IN THE SEMI-FINAL OF THE EUROPEAN CUP.
53,000 FANS SHOUTED AND SCREAMED FOR A GOAL, BUT NONE CAME...
HE MUST SCORE THIS TIME...
NOOOO...
1997-98... BY NOW THOSE FANS HAD GROWN USED TO SUCCESS, AND ANYTHING LESS THAN FIRST PLACE WAS A SHOCK TO THE SYSTEM...
SHARP
TEDDY SHERINGHAM HAD WON NOTHING IN A WONDERFUL CAREER WITH SPURS, AND JUMPED AT THE CHANCE TO JOIN UNITED, WHO WOULDN'T? SOON HE WAS BANGING IN THE GOALS REGULARLY...
UNITED COULD HAVE SUCCESSFULLY DEFENDED THEIR TITLE, BUT...
WE HAVE TO BEAT ARSENAL TODAY...
IT'S EITHER US OR THEM FOR THE TITLE...
AGAINST ARSENAL, AT OLD TRAFFORD IN MARCH, THEY WERE OUTWITTED BY DUTCH MIDFIELDER MARC OVERMARS...
UNITED 0 ARSENAL 1
YOU WEREN'T MARKING HIM!
OVERMARS 11
...AND THE TITLE WAS ON ITS WAY OUT OF OLD TRAFFORD.
IT'S A GOAL FOR THE FRENCH CHAMPIONS...
IN THE EUROPEAN CUP, DEFEAT BY MONACO IN THE QUARTER-FINALS LEFT UNITED, FOR ONCE, STARING AT AN EMPTY TROPHY CABINET...
REDS RULE COMES TO AN END

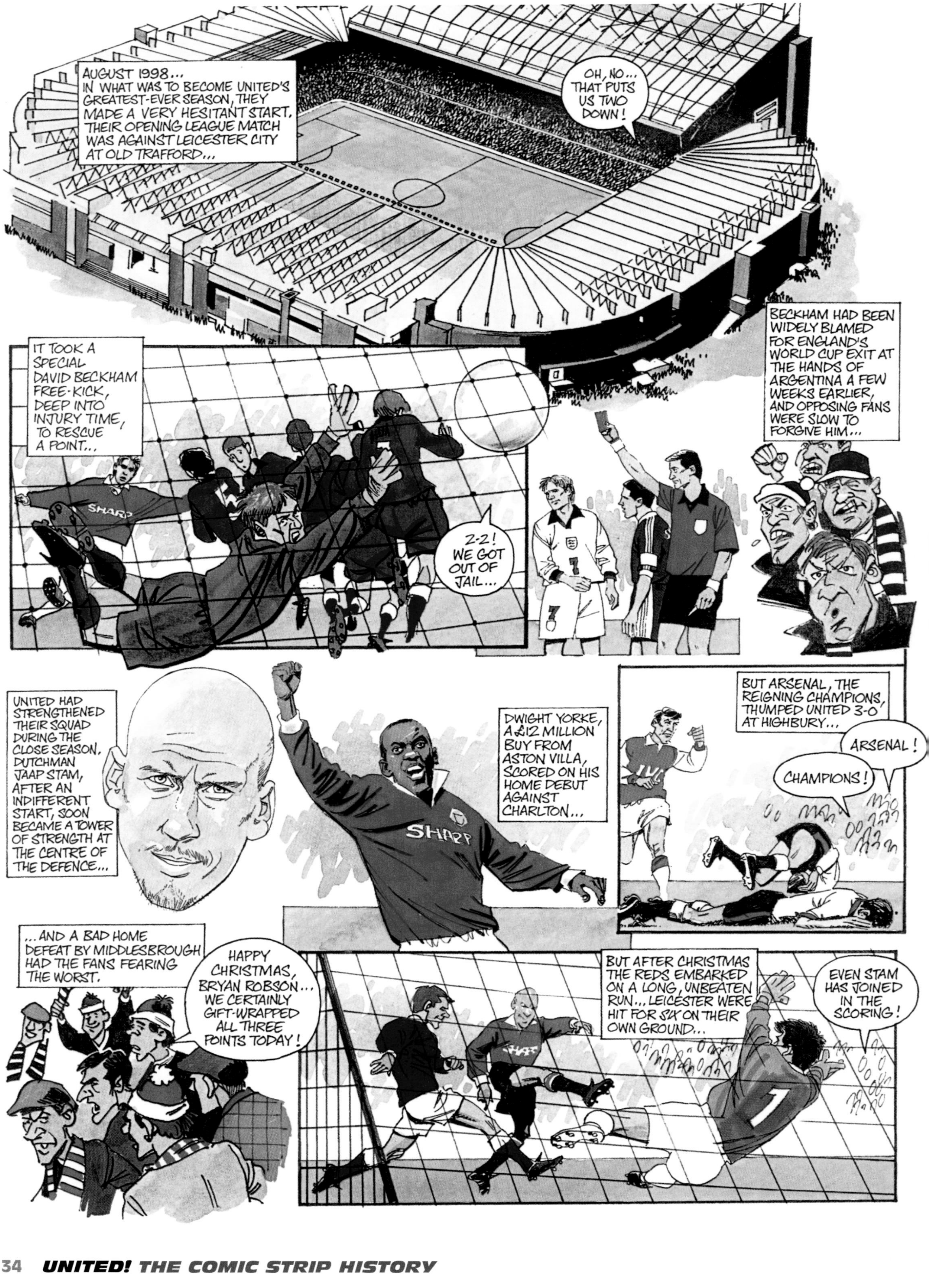
AUGUST 1998... IN WHAT WAS TO BECOME UNITED'S GREATEST-EVER SEASON, THEY MADE A VERY HESITANT START. THEIR OPENING LEAGUE MATCH WAS AGAINST LEICESTER CITY AT OLD TRAFFORD...
OH, NO... THAT PUTS US TWO DOWN!
IT TOOK A SPECIAL DAVID BECKHAM FREE-KICK, DEEP INTO INJURY TIME, TO RESCUE A POINT...
SHARP
2-2! WE GOT OUT OF JAIL...
BECKHAM HAD BEEN WIDELY BLAMED FOR ENGLAND'S WORLD CUP EXIT AT THE HANDS OF ARGENTINA A FEW WEEKS EARLIER, AND OPPOSING FANS WERE SLOW TO FORGIVE HIM...
UNITED HAD STRENGTHENED THEIR SQUAD DURING THE CLOSE SEASON. DUTCHMAN JAAP STAM, AFTER AN INDIFFERENT START, SOON BECAME A TOWER OF STRENGTH AT THE CENTRE OF THE DEFENCE...
DWIGHT YORKE, A £12 MILLION BUY FROM ASTON VILLA, SCORED ON HIS HOME DEBUT AGAINST CHARLTON...
SHARP
BUT ARSENAL, THE REIGNING CHAMPIONS, THUMPED UNITED 3-0 AT HIGHBURY...
ARSENAL!
CHAMPIONS!
...AND A BAD HOME DEFEAT BY MIDDLESBROUGH HAD THE FANS FEARING THE WORST.
HAPPY CHRISTMAS, BRYAN ROBSON... WE CERTAINLY GIFT-WRAPPED ALL THREE POINTS TODAY!
BUT AFTER CHRISTMAS THE REDS EMBARKED ON A LONG, UNBEATEN RUN... LEICESTER WERE HIT FOR SIX ON THEIR OWN GROUND...
EVEN STAM HAS JOINED IN THE SCORING!

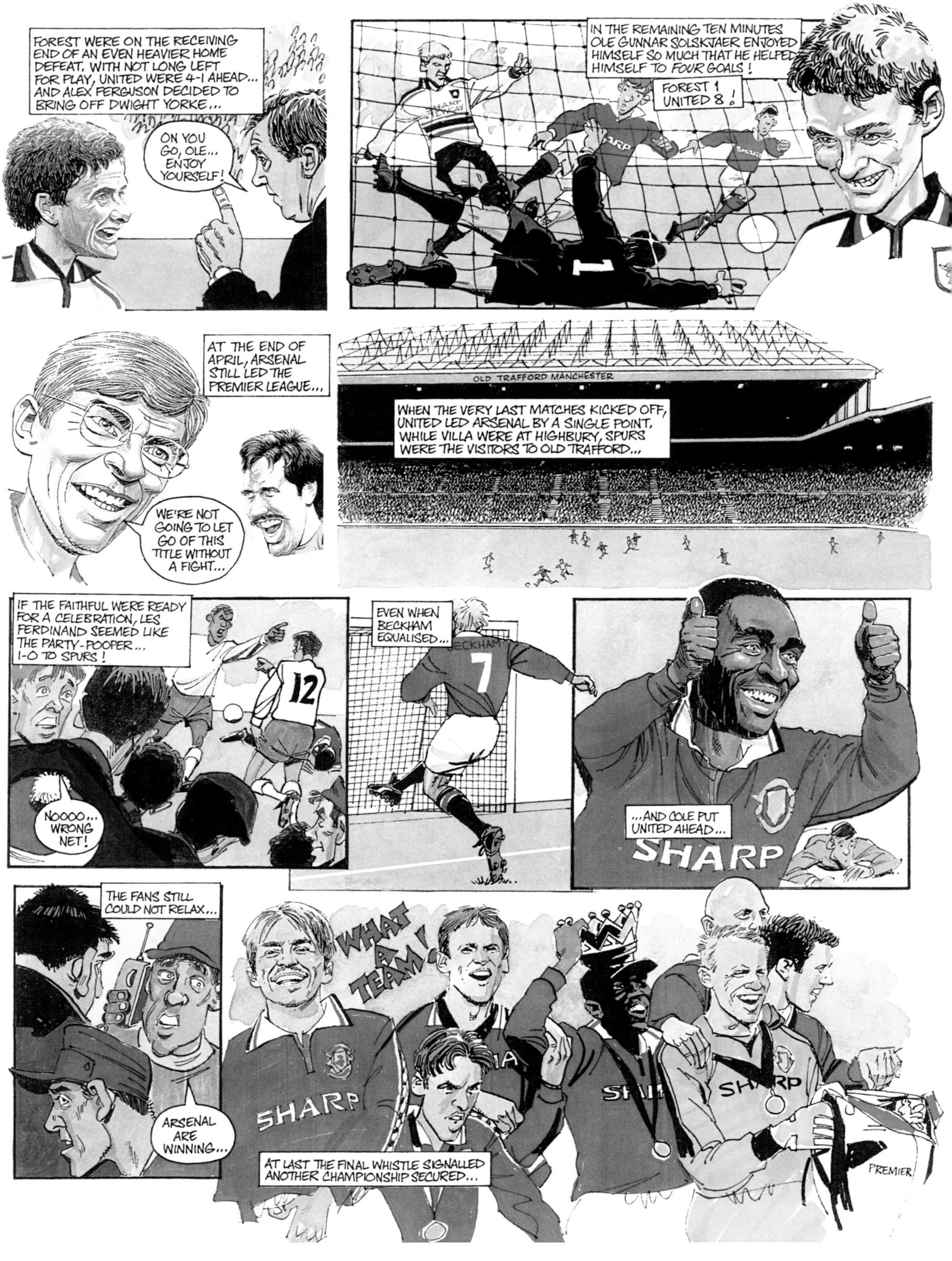
FOREST WERE ON THE RECEIVING END OF AN EVEN HEAVIER HOME DEFEAT. WITH NOT LONG LEFT FOR PLAY, UNITED WERE 4-1 AHEAD... AND ALEX FERGUSON DECIDED TO BRING OFF DWIGHT YORKE...
ON YOU GO, OLE... ENJOY YOURSELF!
IN THE REMAINING TEN MINUTES OLE GUNNAR SOLSKJAER ENJOYED HIMSELF SO MUCH THAT HE HELPED HIMSELF TO FOUR GOALS!
FOREST 1 UNITED 8!
AT THE END OF APRIL, ARSENAL STILL LED THE PREMIER LEAGUE...
WE'RE NOT GOING TO LET GO OF THIS TITLE WITHOUT A FIGHT...
OLD TRAFFORD MANCHESTER
WHEN THE VERY LAST MATCHES KICKED OFF, UNITED LED ARSENAL BY A SINGLE POINT, WHILE VILLA WERE AT HIGHBURY, SPURS WERE THE VISITORS TO OLD TRAFFORD...
IF THE FAITHFUL WERE READY FOR A CELEBRATION, LES FERDINAND SEEMED LIKE THE PARTY-POOPER... 1-0 TO SPURS!
NOOOO... WRONG NET!
EVEN WHEN BECKHAM EQUALISED...
...AND COLE PUT UNITED AHEAD...
SHARP
THE FANS STILL COULD NOT RELAX...
ARSENAL ARE WINNING...
WHAT A TEAM!
SHARP
AT LAST THE FINAL WHISTLE SIGNALLED ANOTHER CHAMPIONSHIP SECURED...
PREMIER

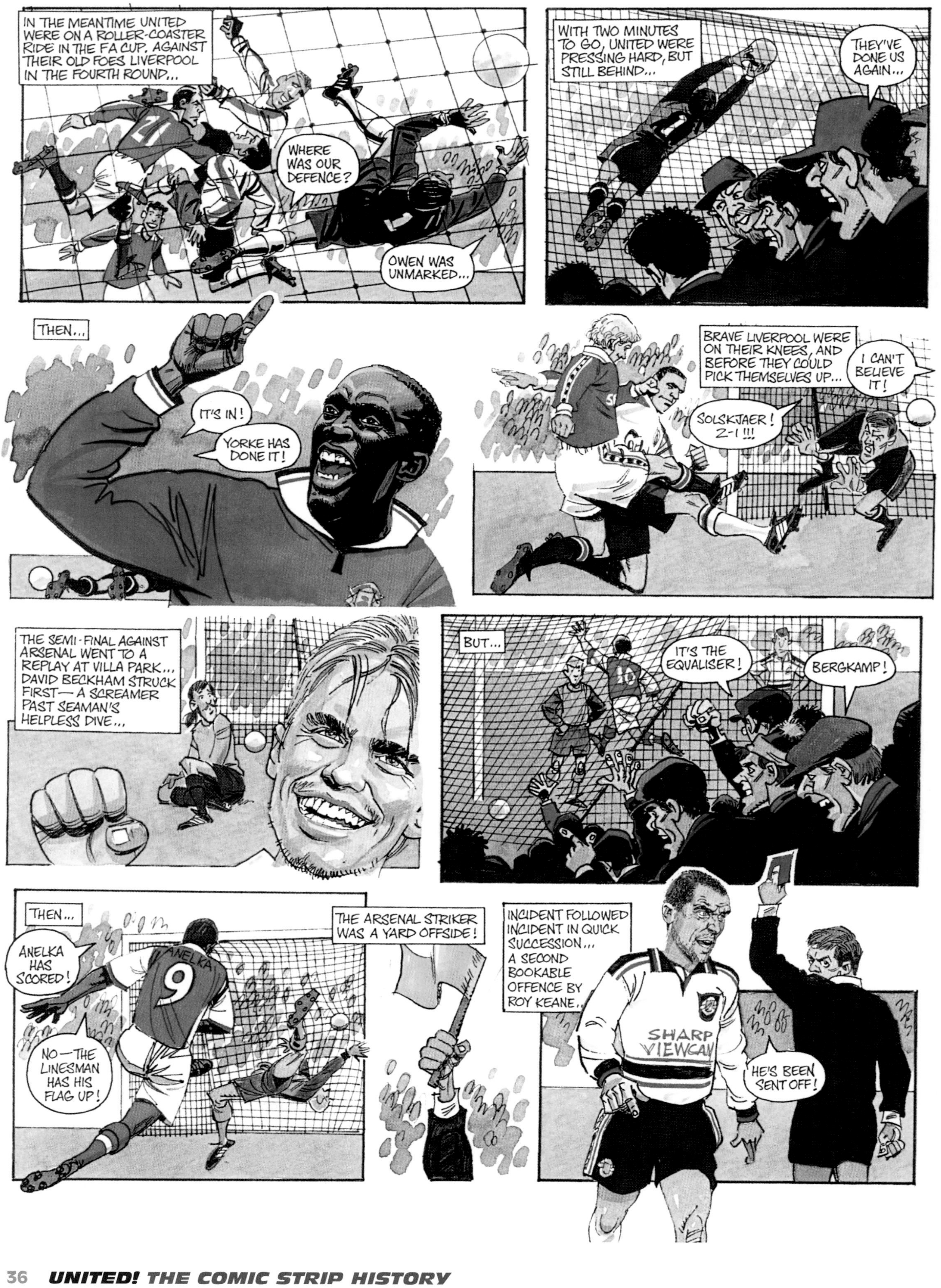
IN THE MEANTIME UNITED WERE ON A ROLLER-COASTER RIDE IN THE FA CUP. AGAINST THEIR OLD FOES LIVERPOOL IN THE FOURTH ROUND...
WHERE WAS OUR DEFENCE?
OWEN WAS UNMARKED...
WITH TWO MINUTES TO GO, UNITED WERE PRESSING HARD, BUT STILL BEHIND...
THEY'VE DONE US AGAIN...
THEN...
IT'S IN!
YORKE HAS DONE IT!
BRAVE LIVERPOOL WERE ON THEIR KNEES, AND BEFORE THEY COULD PICK THEMSELVES UP...
I CAN'T BELIEVE IT!
SOLSKJAER! 2-1!!!
THE SEMI-FINAL AGAINST ARSENAL WENT TO A REPLAY AT VILLA PARK... DAVID BECKHAM STRUCK FIRST— A SCREAMER PAST SEAMAN'S HELPLESS DIVE...
BUT...
IT'S THE EQUALISER!
BERGKAMP!
THEN...
ANELKA HAS SCORED!
NO—THE LINESMAN HAS HIS FLAG UP!
THE ARSENAL STRIKER WAS A YARD OFFSIDE!
INCIDENT FOLLOWED INCIDENT IN QUICK SUCCESSION... A SECOND BOOKABLE OFFENCE BY ROY KEANE...
HE'S BEEN SENT OFF!

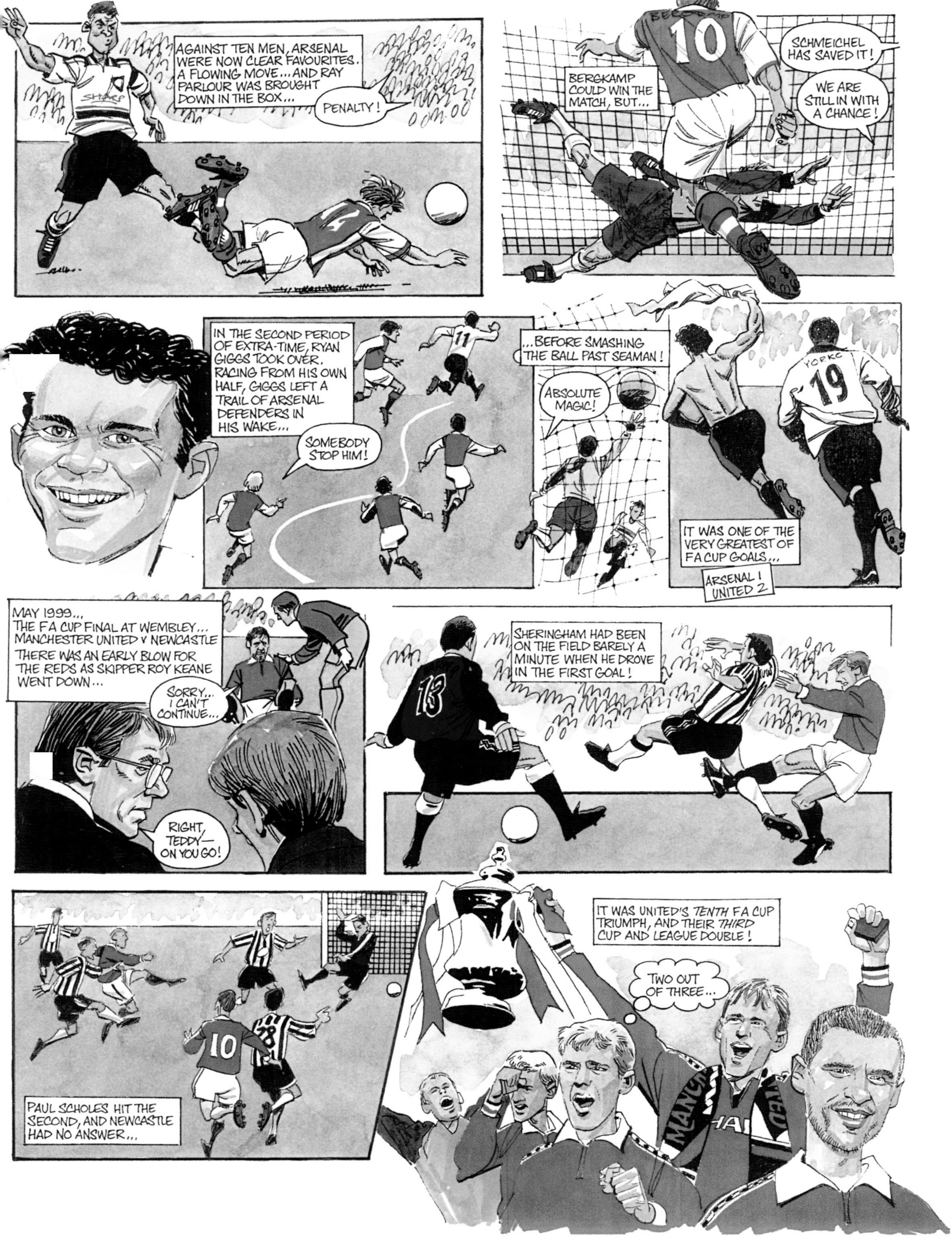
AGAINST TEN MEN, ARSENAL WERE NOW CLEAR FAVOURITES. A FLOWING MOVE... AND RAY PARLOUR WAS BROUGHT DOWN IN THE BOX...
PENALTY!
BERGKAMP COULD WIN THE MATCH, BUT...
SCHMEICHEL HAS SAVED IT!
WE ARE STILL IN WITH A CHANCE!
IN THE SECOND PERIOD OF EXTRA-TIME, RYAN GIGGS TOOK OVER. RACING FROM HIS OWN HALF, GIGGS LEFT A TRAIL OF ARSENAL DEFENDERS IN HIS WAKE...
SOMEBODY STOP HIM!
...BEFORE SMASHING THE BALL PAST SEAMAN!
ABSOLUTE MAGIC!
IT WAS ONE OF THE VERY GREATEST OF FA CUP GOALS...
ARSENAL 1 UNITED 2
MAY 1999...
THE FA CUP FINAL AT WEMBLEY... MANCHESTER UNITED V NEWCASTLE
THERE WAS AN EARLY BLOW FOR THE REDS AS SKIPPER ROY KEANE WENT DOWN...
SORRY... I CAN'T CONTINUE...
RIGHT, TEDDY— ON YOU GO!
SHERINGHAM HAD BEEN ON THE FIELD BARELY A MINUTE WHEN HE DROVE IN THE FIRST GOAL!
PAUL SCHOLES HIT THE SECOND, AND NEWCASTLE HAD NO ANSWER...
IT WAS UNITED'S TENTH FA CUP TRIUMPH, AND THEIR THIRD CUP AND LEAGUE DOUBLE!
TWO OUT OF THREE...

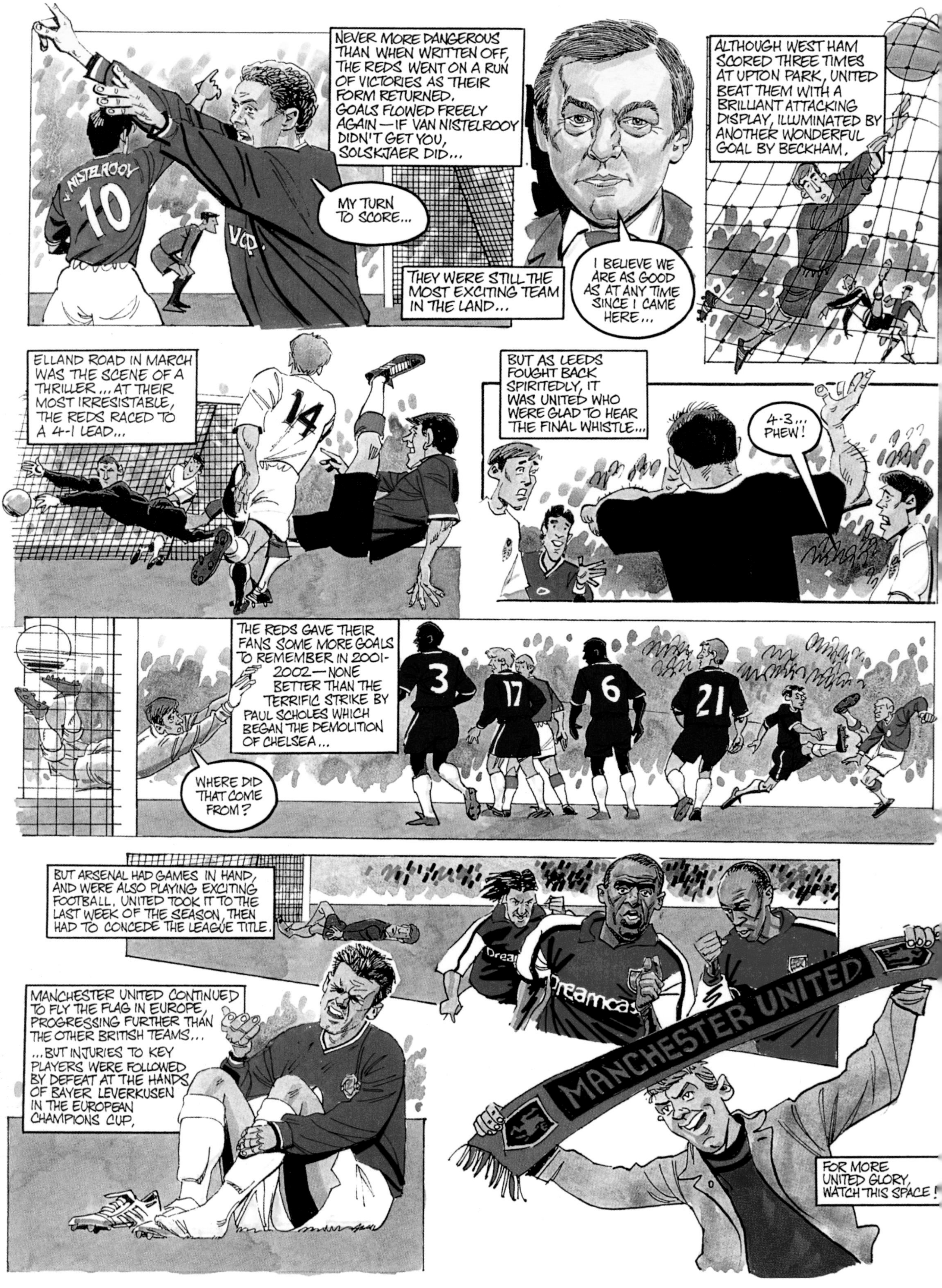
NEVER MORE DANGEROUS THAN WHEN WRITTEN OFF, THE REDS WENT ON A RUN OF VICTORIES AS THEIR FORM RETURNED. GOALS FLOWED FREELY AGAIN — IF VAN NISTELROOY DIDN'T GET YOU, SOLSKJAER DID...
NISTELROOY
10
MY TURN TO SCORE...
THEY WERE STILL THE MOST EXCITING TEAM IN THE LAND...
I BELIEVE WE ARE AS GOOD AS AT ANY TIME SINCE I CAME HERE...
ALTHOUGH WEST HAM SCORED THREE TIMES AT UPTON PARK, UNITED BEAT THEM WITH A BRILLIANT ATTACKING DISPLAY, ILLUMINATED BY ANOTHER WONDERFUL GOAL BY BECKHAM.
ELLAND ROAD IN MARCH WAS THE SCENE OF A THRILLER... AT THEIR MOST IRRESISTABLE, THE REDS RACED TO A 4-1 LEAD...
14
BUT AS LEEDS FOUGHT BACK SPIRITEDLY, IT WAS UNITED WHO WERE GLAD TO HEAR THE FINAL WHISTLE...
4-3... PHEW!
THE REDS GAVE THEIR FANS SOME MORE GOALS TO REMEMBER IN 2001-2002 — NONE BETTER THAN THE TERRIFIC STRIKE BY PAUL SCHOLES WHICH BEGAN THE DEMOLITION OF CHELSEA...
3
17
6
21
WHERE DID THAT COME FROM?
BUT ARSENAL HAD GAMES IN HAND, AND WERE ALSO PLAYING EXCITING FOOTBALL. UNITED TOOK IT TO THE LAST WEEK OF THE SEASON, THEN HAD TO CONCEDE THE LEAGUE TITLE.
MANCHESTER UNITED CONTINUED TO FLY THE FLAG IN EUROPE, PROGRESSING FURTHER THAN THE OTHER BRITISH TEAMS...
...BUT INJURIES TO KEY PLAYERS WERE FOLLOWED BY DEFEAT AT THE HANDS OF BAYER LEVERKUSEN IN THE EUROPEAN CHAMPIONS CUP.
MANCHESTER UNITED
FOR MORE UNITED GLORY, WATCH THIS SPACE!

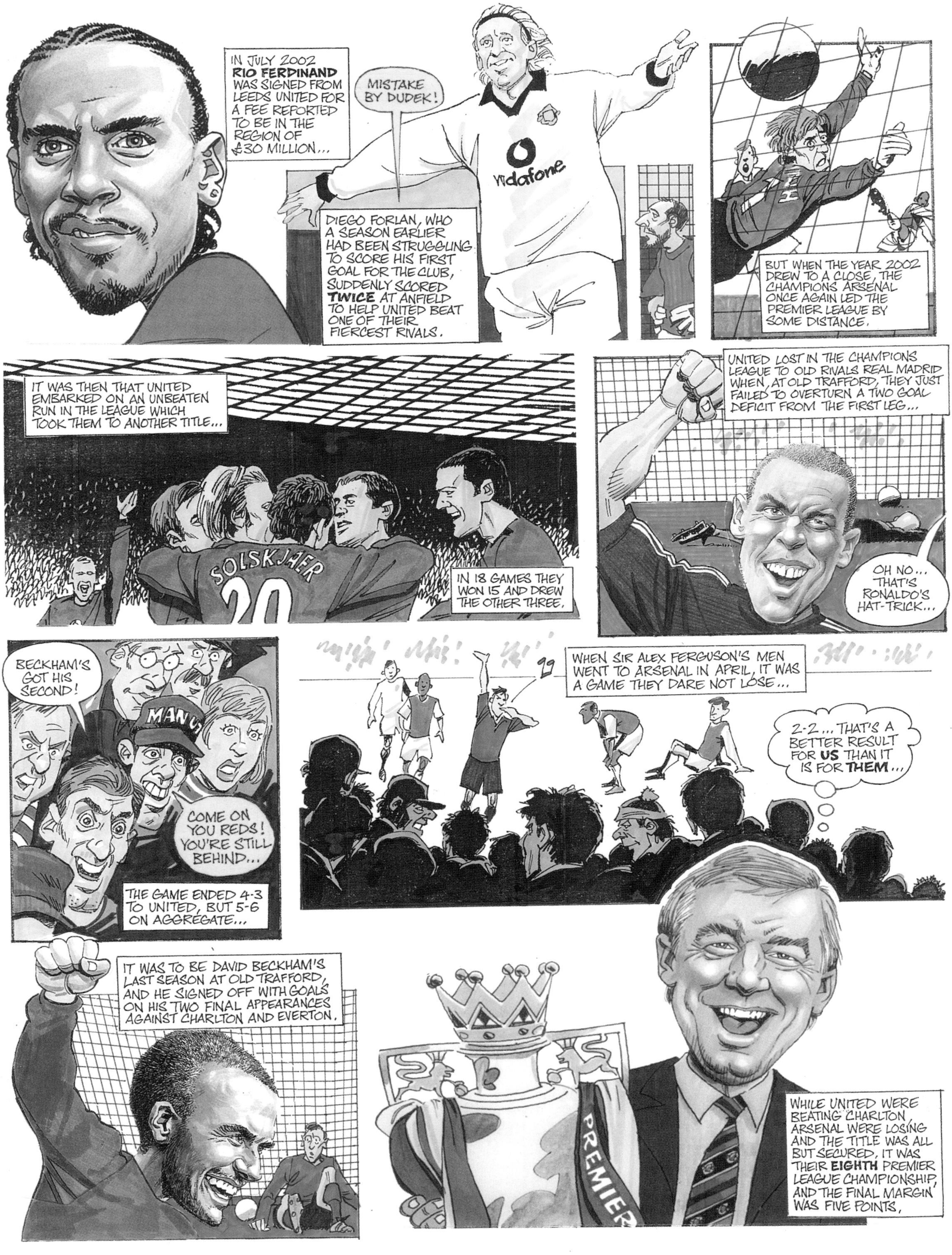
IN JULY 2002 **RIO FERDINAND** WAS SIGNED FROM LEEDS UNITED FOR A FEE REPORTED TO BE IN THE REGION OF £30 MILLION...
MISTAKE BY DUDEK!
vodafone
DIEGO FORLAN, WHO A SEASON EARLIER HAD BEEN STRUGGLING TO SCORE HIS FIRST GOAL FOR THE CLUB, SUDDENLY SCORED **TWICE** AT ANFIELD TO HELP UNITED BEAT ONE OF THEIR FIERCEST RIVALS.
BUT WHEN THE YEAR 2002 DREW TO A CLOSE, THE CHAMPIONS ARSENAL ONCE AGAIN LED THE PREMIER LEAGUE BY SOME DISTANCE.
IT WAS THEN THAT UNITED EMBARKED ON AN UNBEATEN RUN IN THE LEAGUE WHICH TOOK THEM TO ANOTHER TITLE...
SOLSKJAER 20
IN 18 GAMES THEY WON 15 AND DREW THE OTHER THREE.
UNITED LOST IN THE CHAMPIONS LEAGUE TO OLD RIVALS REAL MADRID WHEN, AT OLD TRAFFORD, THEY JUST FAILED TO OVERTURN A TWO GOAL DEFICIT FROM THE FIRST LEG...
OH NO... THAT'S RONALDO'S HAT-TRICK...
BECKHAM'S GOT HIS SECOND!
MAN U
COME ON YOU REDS! YOU'RE STILL BEHIND...
THE GAME ENDED 4-3 TO UNITED, BUT 5-6 ON AGGREGATE...
WHEN SIR ALEX FERGUSON'S MEN WENT TO ARSENAL IN APRIL, IT WAS A GAME THEY DARE NOT LOSE...
2-2... THAT'S A BETTER RESULT FOR **US** THAN IT IS FOR **THEM**...
IT WAS TO BE DAVID BECKHAM'S LAST SEASON AT OLD TRAFFORD, AND HE SIGNED OFF WITH GOALS ON HIS TWO FINAL APPEARANCES AGAINST CHARLTON AND EVERTON.
PREMIER
WHILE UNITED WERE BEATING CHARLTON, ARSENAL WERE LOSING AND THE TITLE WAS ALL BUT SECURED. IT WAS THEIR **EIGHTH** PREMIER LEAGUE CHAMPIONSHIP, AND THE FINAL MARGIN WAS FIVE POINTS.

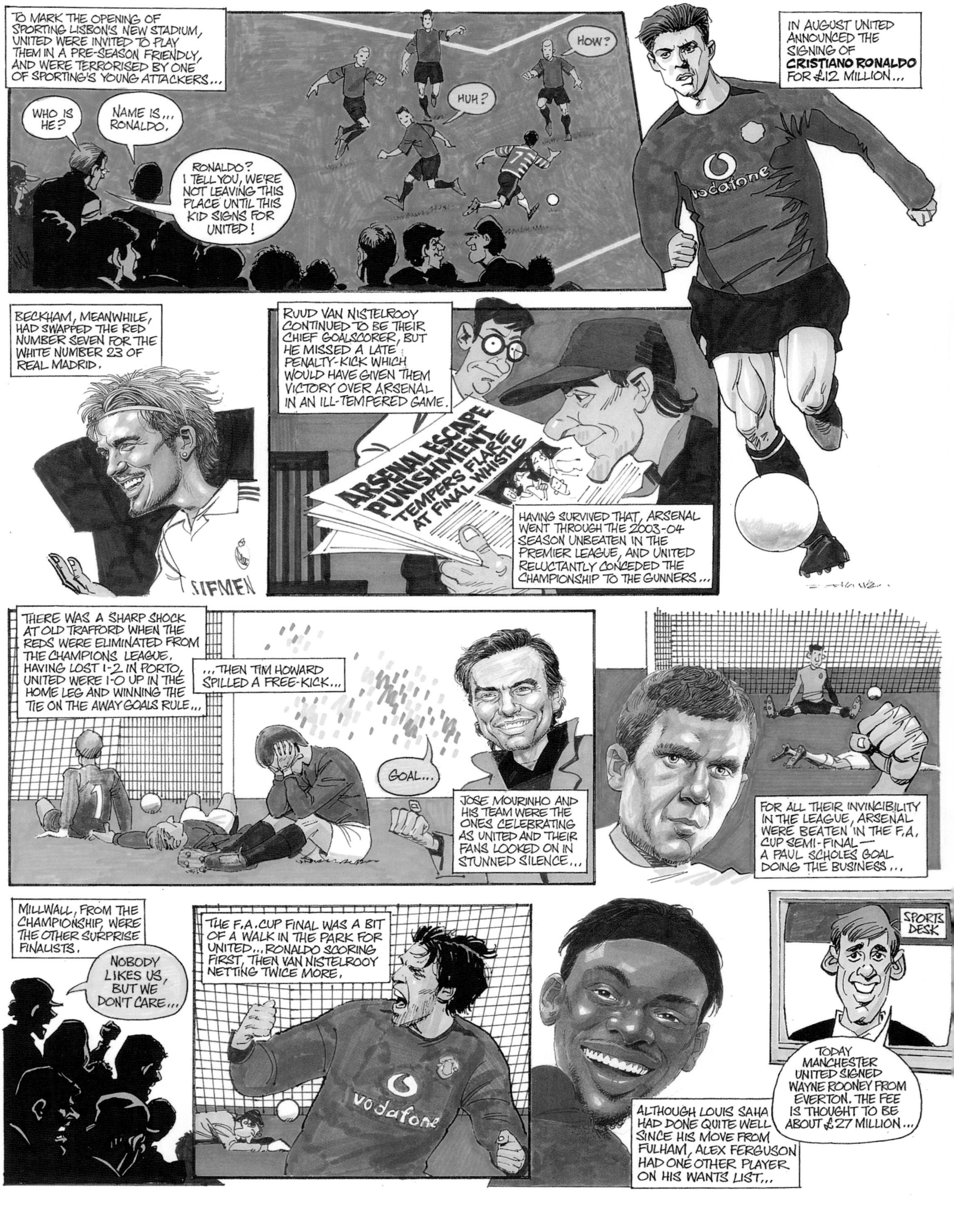
TO MARK THE OPENING OF SPORTING LISBON'S NEW STADIUM, UNITED WERE INVITED TO PLAY THEM IN A PRE-SEASON FRIENDLY, AND WERE TERRORISED BY ONE OF SPORTING'S YOUNG ATTACKERS...
HOW?
HUH?
WHO IS HE?
NAME IS... RONALDO.
RONALDO? I TELL YOU, WE'RE NOT LEAVING THIS PLACE UNTIL THIS KID SIGNS FOR UNITED!
IN AUGUST UNITED ANNOUNCED THE SIGNING OF CRISTIANO RONALDO FOR £12 MILLION...
vodafone
BECKHAM, MEANWHILE, HAD SWAPPED THE RED NUMBER SEVEN FOR THE WHITE NUMBER 23 OF REAL MADRID.
SIEMEN
RUUD VAN NISTELROOY CONTINUED TO BE THEIR CHIEF GOALSCORER, BUT HE MISSED A LATE PENALTY-KICK WHICH WOULD HAVE GIVEN THEM VICTORY OVER ARSENAL IN AN ILL-TEMPERED GAME.
ARSENAL ESCAPE PUNISHMENT
TEMPERS FLARE AT FINAL WHISTLE
HAVING SURVIVED THAT, ARSENAL WENT THROUGH THE 2003-04 SEASON UNBEATEN IN THE PREMIER LEAGUE, AND UNITED RELUCTANTLY CONCEDED THE CHAMPIONSHIP TO THE GUNNERS...
THERE WAS A SHARP SHOCK AT OLD TRAFFORD WHEN THE REDS WERE ELIMINATED FROM THE CHAMPIONS LEAGUE. HAVING LOST 1-2 IN PORTO, UNITED WERE 1-0 UP IN THE HOME LEG AND WINNING THE TIE ON THE AWAY GOALS RULE...
...THEN TIM HOWARD SPILLED A FREE-KICK...
GOAL...
JOSE MOURINHO AND HIS TEAM WERE THE ONES CELEBRATING AS UNITED AND THEIR FANS LOOKED ON IN STUNNED SILENCE...
FOR ALL THEIR INVINCIBILITY IN THE LEAGUE, ARSENAL WERE BEATEN IN THE F.A. CUP SEMI-FINAL — A PAUL SCHOLES GOAL DOING THE BUSINESS...
MILLWALL, FROM THE CHAMPIONSHIP, WERE THE OTHER SURPRISE FINALISTS.
NOBODY LIKES US, BUT WE DON'T CARE...
THE F.A. CUP FINAL WAS A BIT OF A WALK IN THE PARK FOR UNITED... RONALDO SCORING FIRST, THEN VAN NISTELROOY NETTING TWICE MORE.
vodafone
ALTHOUGH LOUIS SAHA HAD DONE QUITE WELL SINCE HIS MOVE FROM FULHAM, ALEX FERGUSON HAD ONE OTHER PLAYER ON HIS WANTS LIST...
SPORTS DESK
TODAY MANCHESTER UNITED SIGNED WAYNE ROONEY FROM EVERTON. THE FEE IS THOUGHT TO BE ABOUT £27 MILLION...

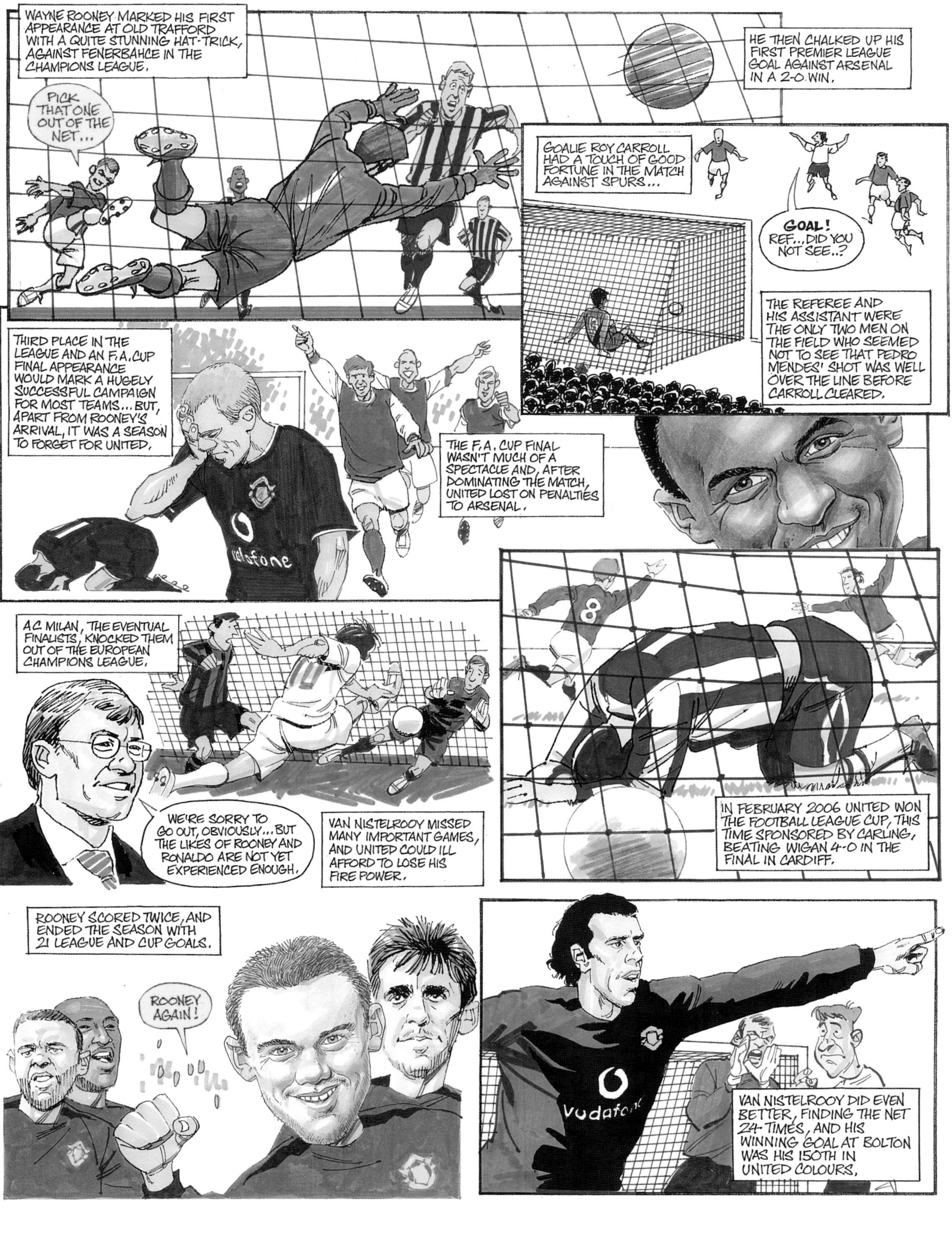
WAYNE ROONEY MARKED HIS FIRST APPEARANCE AT OLD TRAFFORD WITH A QUITE STUNNING HAT-TRICK, AGAINST FENERBAHCE IN THE CHAMPIONS LEAGUE.
PICK THAT ONE OUT OF THE NET...
HE THEN CHALKED UP HIS FIRST PREMIER LEAGUE GOAL AGAINST ARSENAL IN A 2-0 WIN.
GOALIE ROY CARROLL HAD A TOUCH OF GOOD FORTUNE IN THE MATCH AGAINST SPURS...
GOAL! REF...DID YOU NOT SEE..?
THE REFEREE AND HIS ASSISTANT WERE THE ONLY TWO MEN ON THE FIELD WHO SEEMED NOT TO SEE THAT PEDRO MENDES' SHOT WAS WELL OVER THE LINE BEFORE CARROLL CLEARED.
THIRD PLACE IN THE LEAGUE AND AN F.A. CUP FINAL APPEARANCE WOULD MARK A HUGELY SUCCESSFUL CAMPAIGN FOR MOST TEAMS... BUT, APART FROM ROONEY'S ARRIVAL, IT WAS A SEASON TO FORGET FOR UNITED.
THE F.A. CUP FINAL WASN'T MUCH OF A SPECTACLE AND, AFTER DOMINATING THE MATCH, UNITED LOST ON PENALTIES TO ARSENAL.
vodafone
AC MILAN, THE EVENTUAL FINALISTS, KNOCKED THEM OUT OF THE EUROPEAN CHAMPIONS LEAGUE.
WE'RE SORRY TO GO OUT, OBVIOUSLY... BUT THE LIKES OF ROONEY AND RONALDO ARE NOT YET EXPERIENCED ENOUGH.
VAN NISTELROOY MISSED MANY IMPORTANT GAMES, AND UNITED COULD ILL AFFORD TO LOSE HIS FIRE POWER.
IN FEBRUARY 2006 UNITED WON THE FOOTBALL LEAGUE CUP, THIS TIME SPONSORED BY CARLING, BEATING WIGAN 4-0 IN THE FINAL IN CARDIFF.
ROONEY SCORED TWICE, AND ENDED THE SEASON WITH 21 LEAGUE AND CUP GOALS.
ROONEY AGAIN!
VAN NISTELROOY DID EVEN BETTER, FINDING THE NET 24 TIMES, AND HIS WINNING GOAL AT BOLTON WAS HIS 150TH IN UNITED COLOURS.

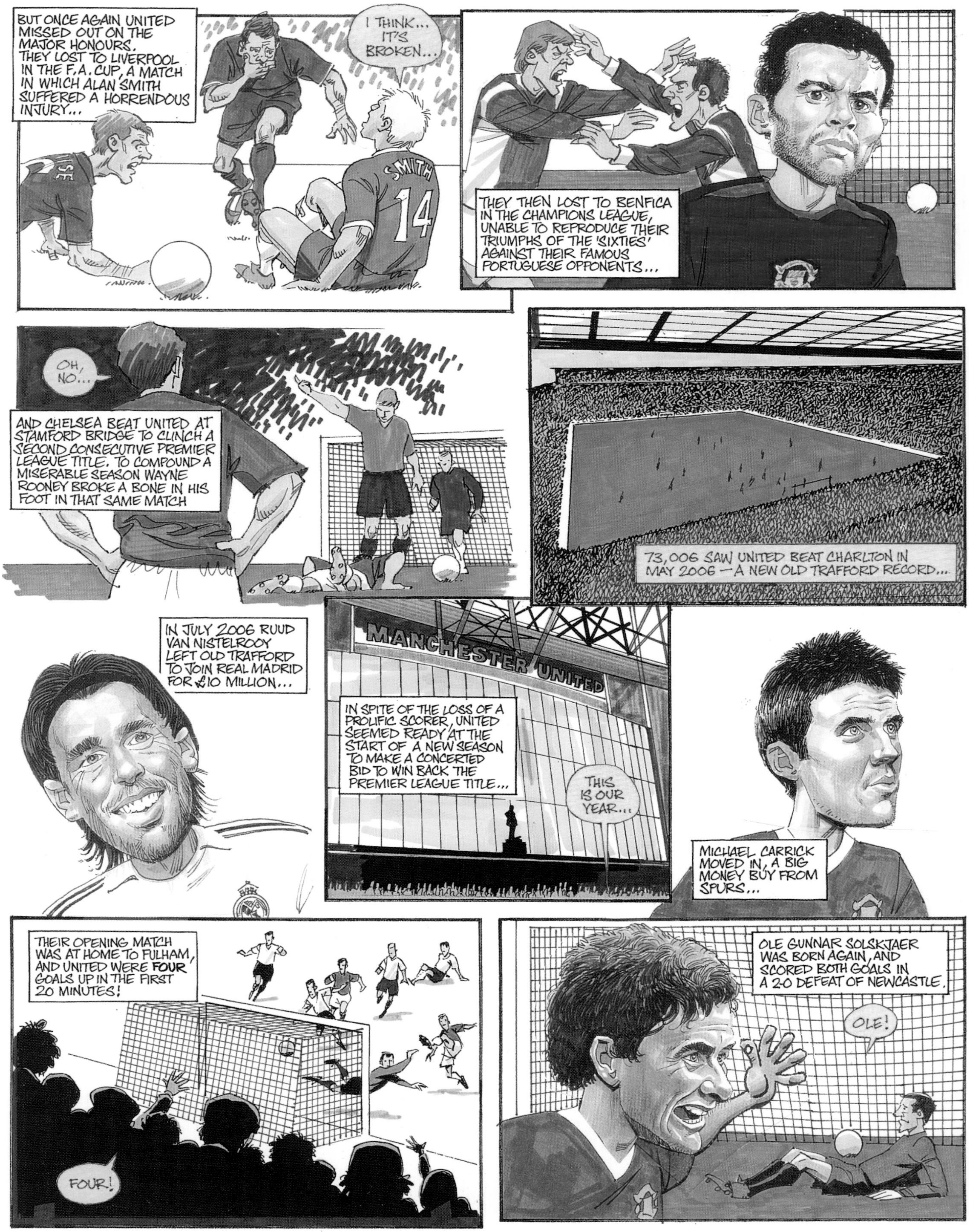
BUT ONCE AGAIN UNITED MISSED OUT ON THE MAJOR HONOURS. THEY LOST TO LIVERPOOL IN THE F.A. CUP, A MATCH IN WHICH ALAN SMITH SUFFERED A HORRENDOUS INJURY...
I THINK... IT'S BROKEN...
SMITH 14
THEY THEN LOST TO BENFICA IN THE CHAMPIONS LEAGUE, UNABLE TO REPRODUCE THEIR TRIUMPHS OF THE 'SIXTIES' AGAINST THEIR FAMOUS PORTUGUESE OPPONENTS...
OH, NO...
AND CHELSEA BEAT UNITED AT STAMFORD BRIDGE TO CLINCH A SECOND CONSECUTIVE PREMIER LEAGUE TITLE. TO COMPOUND A MISERABLE SEASON WAYNE ROONEY BROKE A BONE IN HIS FOOT IN THAT SAME MATCH
73,006 SAW UNITED BEAT CHARLTON IN MAY 2006 — A NEW OLD TRAFFORD RECORD...
IN JULY 2006 RUUD VAN NISTELROOY LEFT OLD TRAFFORD TO JOIN REAL MADRID FOR £10 MILLION...
MANCHESTER UNITED
IN SPITE OF THE LOSS OF A PROLIFIC SCORER, UNITED SEEMED READY AT THE START OF A NEW SEASON TO MAKE A CONCERTED BID TO WIN BACK THE PREMIER LEAGUE TITLE...
THIS IS OUR YEAR...
MICHAEL CARRICK MOVED IN, A BIG MONEY BUY FROM SPURS...
THEIR OPENING MATCH WAS AT HOME TO FULHAM, AND UNITED WERE **FOUR** GOALS UP IN THE FIRST 20 MINUTES!
FOUR!
OLE GUNNAR SOLSKJAER WAS BORN AGAIN, AND SCORED BOTH GOALS IN A 2-0 DEFEAT OF NEWCASTLE.
OLE!

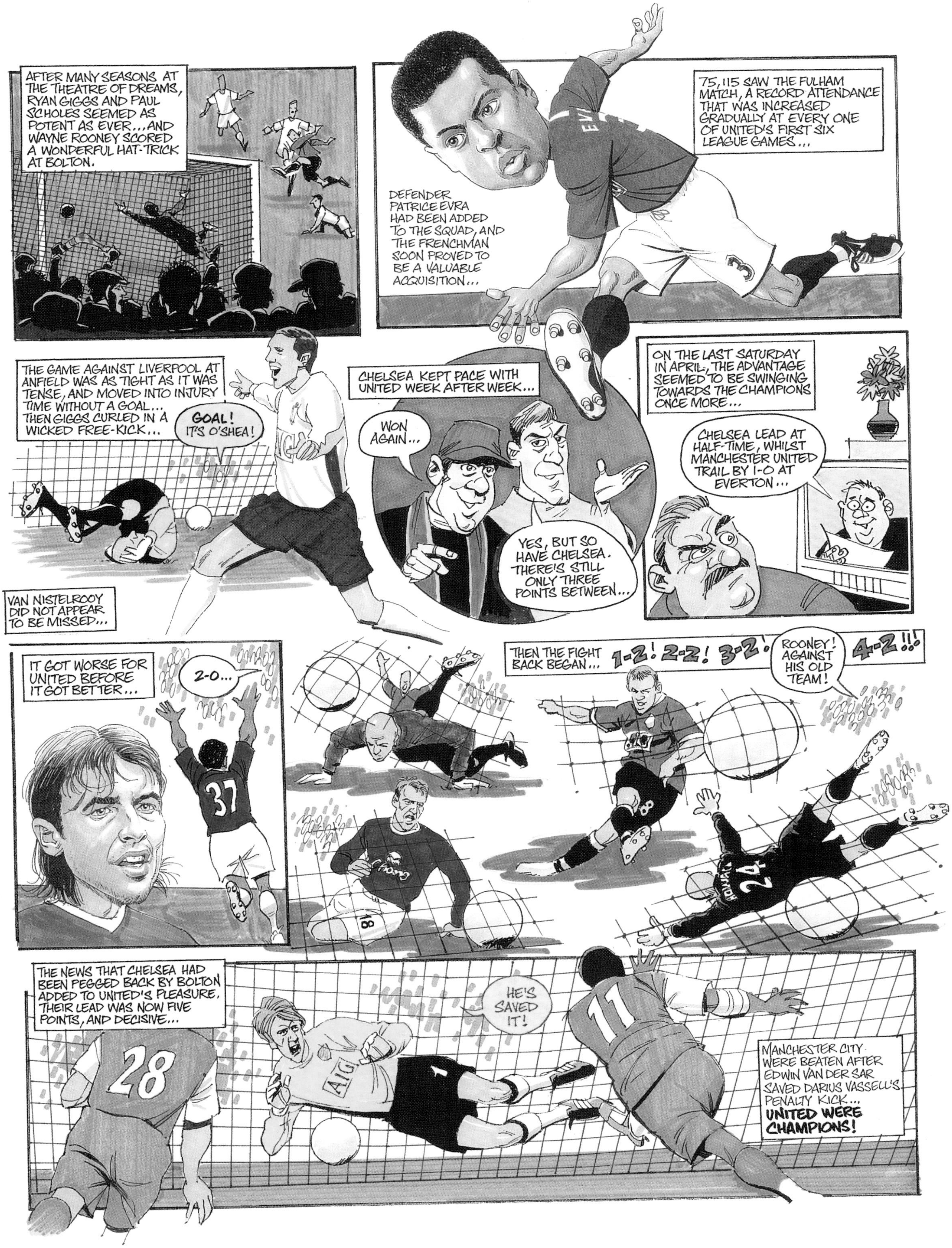
AFTER MANY SEASONS AT THE THEATRE OF DREAMS, RYAN GIGGS AND PAUL SCHOLES SEEMED AS POTENT AS EVER..., AND WAYNE ROONEY SCORED A WONDERFUL HAT-TRICK AT BOLTON.
75,115 SAW THE FULHAM MATCH, A RECORD ATTENDANCE THAT WAS INCREASED GRADUALLY AT EVERY ONE OF UNITED'S FIRST SIX LEAGUE GAMES...
DEFENDER PATRICE EVRA HAD BEEN ADDED TO THE SQUAD, AND THE FRENCHMAN SOON PROVED TO BE A VALUABLE ACQUISITION...
THE GAME AGAINST LIVERPOOL AT ANFIELD WAS AS TIGHT AS IT WAS TENSE, AND MOVED INTO INJURY TIME WITHOUT A GOAL... THEN GIGGS CURLED IN A WICKED FREE-KICK...
GOAL! IT'S O'SHEA!
VAN NISTELROOY DID NOT APPEAR TO BE MISSED...
CHELSEA KEPT PACE WITH UNITED WEEK AFTER WEEK...
WON AGAIN...
YES, BUT SO HAVE CHELSEA. THERE'S STILL ONLY THREE POINTS BETWEEN...
ON THE LAST SATURDAY IN APRIL, THE ADVANTAGE SEEMED TO BE SWINGING TOWARDS THE CHAMPIONS ONCE MORE...
CHELSEA LEAD AT HALF-TIME, WHILST MANCHESTER UNITED TRAIL BY 1-0 AT EVERTON...
IT GOT WORSE FOR UNITED BEFORE IT GOT BETTER...
2-0...
THEN THE FIGHT BACK BEGAN... 1-2! 2-2! 3-2!
ROONEY! AGAINST HIS OLD TEAM!
4-2!!!
THE NEWS THAT CHELSEA HAD BEEN PEGGED BACK BY BOLTON ADDED TO UNITED'S PLEASURE, THEIR LEAD WAS NOW FIVE POINTS, AND DECISIVE...
HE'S SAVED IT!
MANCHESTER CITY WERE BEATEN AFTER EDWIN VAN DER SAR SAVED DARIUS VASSELL'S PENALTY KICK... UNITED WERE CHAMPIONS!

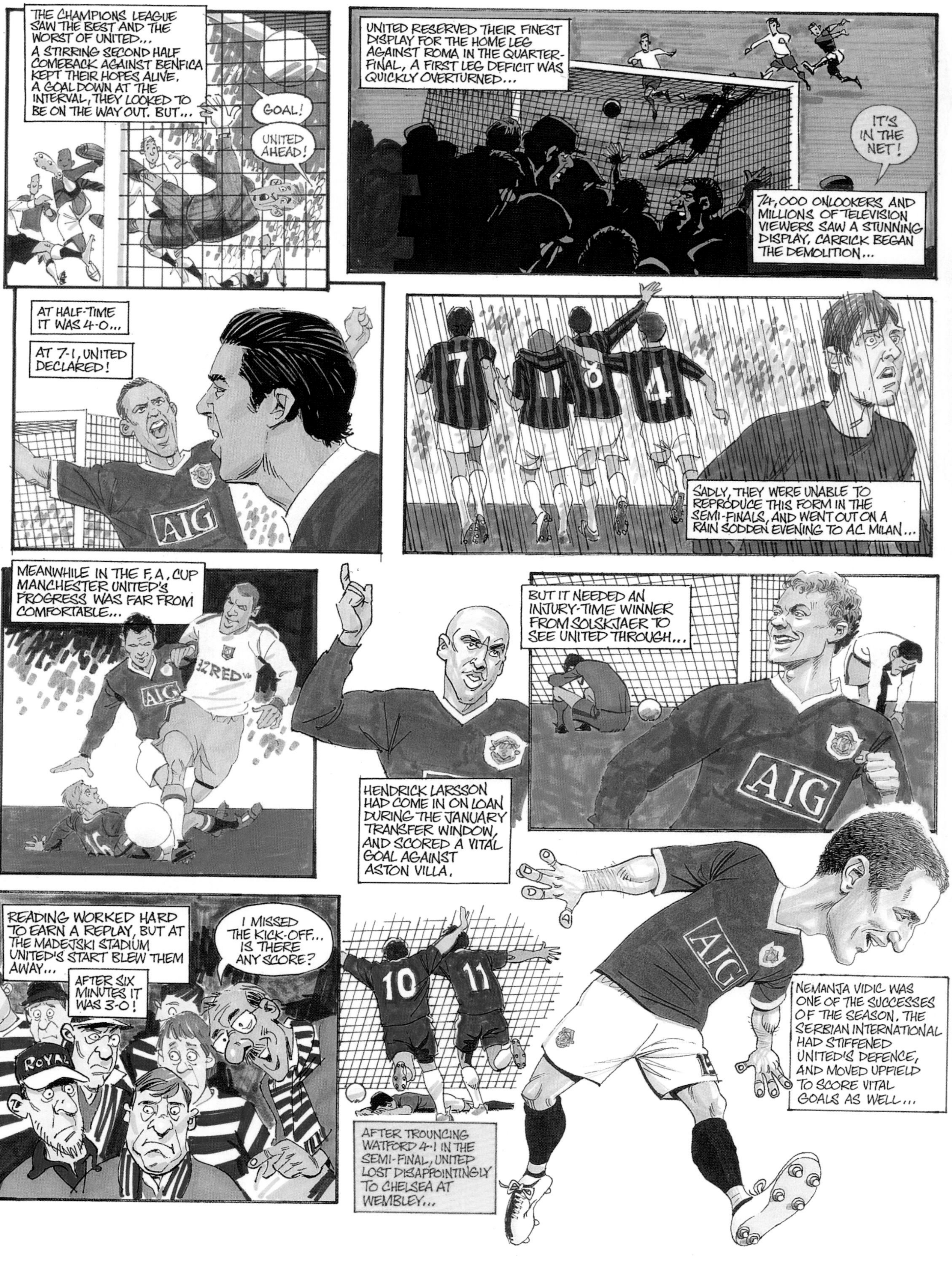

THE CHAMPIONS LEAGUE SAW THE BEST AND THE WORST OF UNITED... A STIRRING SECOND HALF COMEBACK AGAINST BENFICA KEPT THEIR HOPES ALIVE. A GOAL DOWN AT THE INTERVAL, THEY LOOKED TO BE ON THE WAY OUT. BUT...
GOAL!
UNITED AHEAD!
UNITED RESERVED THEIR FINEST DISPLAY FOR THE HOME LEG AGAINST ROMA IN THE QUARTER-FINAL, A FIRST LEG DEFICIT WAS QUICKLY OVERTURNED...
IT'S IN THE NET!
74,000 ONLOOKERS AND MILLIONS OF TELEVISION VIEWERS SAW A STUNNING DISPLAY. CARRICK BEGAN THE DEMOLITION...
AT HALF-TIME IT WAS 4-0...
AT 7-1, UNITED DECLARED!
AIG
SADLY, THEY WERE UNABLE TO REPRODUCE THIS FORM IN THE SEMI-FINALS, AND WENT OUT ON A RAIN SODDEN EVENING TO AC MILAN...
MEANWHILE IN THE F.A. CUP MANCHESTER UNITED'S PROGRESS WAS FAR FROM COMFORTABLE...
HENDRICK LARSSON HAD COME IN ON LOAN DURING THE JANUARY TRANSFER WINDOW, AND SCORED A VITAL GOAL AGAINST ASTON VILLA.
BUT IT NEEDED AN INJURY-TIME WINNER FROM SOLSKJAER TO SEE UNITED THROUGH...
READING WORKED HARD TO EARN A REPLAY, BUT AT THE MADEJSKI STADIUM UNITED'S START BLEW THEM AWAY...
AFTER SIX MINUTES IT WAS 3-0!
I MISSED THE KICK-OFF... IS THERE ANY SCORE?
ROYAL
AFTER TROUNCING WATFORD 4-1 IN THE SEMI-FINAL, UNITED LOST DISAPPOINTINGLY TO CHELSEA AT WEMBLEY...
NEMANJA VIDIC WAS ONE OF THE SUCCESSES OF THE SEASON. THE SERBIAN INTERNATIONAL HAD STIFFENED UNITED'S DEFENCE, AND MOVED UPFIELD TO SCORE VITAL GOALS AS WELL...

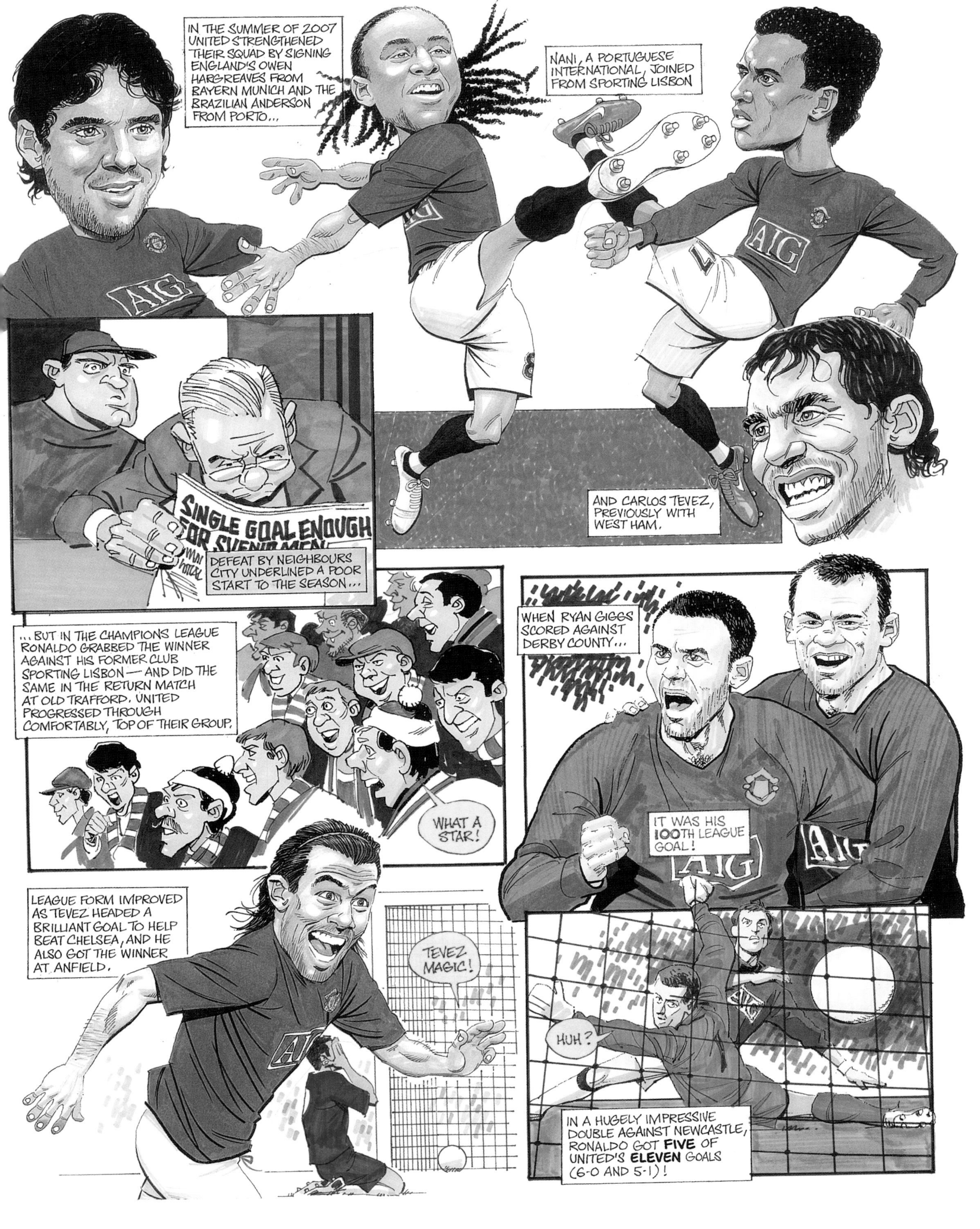

IN THE SUMMER OF 2007 UNITED STRENGTHENED THEIR SQUAD BY SIGNING ENGLAND'S OWEN HARGREAVES FROM BAYERN MUNICH AND THE BRAZILIAN ANDERSON FROM PORTO...
NANI, A PORTUGUESE INTERNATIONAL, JOINED FROM SPORTING LISBON
AND CARLOS TEVEZ, PREVIOUSLY WITH WEST HAM.
SINGLE GOAL ENOUGH FOR SVENIRMEN
DEFEAT BY NEIGHBOURS CITY UNDERLINED A POOR START TO THE SEASON...
...BUT IN THE CHAMPIONS LEAGUE RONALDO GRABBED THE WINNER AGAINST HIS FORMER CLUB SPORTING LISBON — AND DID THE SAME IN THE RETURN MATCH AT OLD TRAFFORD. UNITED PROGRESSED THROUGH COMFORTABLY, TOP OF THEIR GROUP.
WHAT A STAR!
WHEN RYAN GIGGS SCORED AGAINST DERBY COUNTY...
IT WAS HIS 100TH LEAGUE GOAL!
LEAGUE FORM IMPROVED AS TEVEZ HEADED A BRILLIANT GOAL TO HELP BEAT CHELSEA, AND HE ALSO GOT THE WINNER AT ANFIELD.
TEVEZ MAGIC!
HUH?
IN A HUGELY IMPRESSIVE DOUBLE AGAINST NEWCASTLE, RONALDO GOT FIVE OF UNITED'S ELEVEN GOALS (6-0 AND 5-1)!

# FACTS & FIGURES

## All-time top goalscorers

| | | |
|---|---|---|
| 1. | Sir Bobby Charlton (1956-73) | 249 |
| 2. | Denis Law (1962-73) | 237 |
| 3. | Jack Rowley (1937-55) | 211 |
| 4. | Dennis Viollet (1953-62) | 179 |
| 5. | George Best (1963-74) | 179 |
| 6. | Joe Spence (1919-33) | 168 |
| 7. | Mark Hughes (1983-86 & 1988-95) | 163 |
| 8. | Ruud van Nistelrooy (2001-06) | 150 |
| 9. | Stan Pearson (1937-54) | 148 |
| 10. | David Herd (1961-68) | 145 |

## Record win

10-0 v Anderlecht (h), European Cup preliminary round second leg, 26th September 1956

## Record defeat

0-7 v Blackburn Rovers (a), First Division, 10th April 1926
0-7 v Aston Villa (a), First Division, 27th December 1930
0-7 v Wolves (a), First Division, 26th December 1931

## Most goals in a match by one player

6 Harold Halse, 25th September 1911, Manchester United 8 Swindon 4 (Charity Shield)`
6 George Best, 7th February 1970, Northampton 2 Manchester United 8 (FA Cup 5th rd)
5 Jack Rowley, 12th February 1949, Manchester United 8 Yeovil 0 (FA Cup 5th rd)
5 Andy Cole, 4th March 1995, Manchester United 9 Ipswich 0 (Premiership)

## Most Premiership appearances

| | | |
|---|---|---|
| 1. | Ryan Giggs (1991- ) | 495 |
| 2. | Paul Scholes (1994- ) | 395 |
| 3. | Gary Neville (1992- ) | 364 |
| 4. | Roy Keane (1993-2006) | 326 |
| 5. | Denis Irwin (1990-2002) | 296 |

## HONOURS

**First Division championship:** 1907/08, 1910/11, 1951/52, 1955/56, 1956/57, 1964/65, 1966/67

**Second Division championship:** 1935/36, 1974/75

**Premiership:** 1992/93, 1993/94, 1995/96, 1996/97, 1998/99, 1999/2000, 2000/01, 2002/03, 2006/07, 2007/08

**FA Cup:** 1909, 1948, 1963, 1977, 1983, 1985, 1990, 1994, 1996, 1999, 2004

**League Cup:** 1992, 2006

**Charity Shield/Community Shield:** 1908, 1911, 1952, 1956, 1957, 1965*, 1967*, 1977*, 1983, 1990*, 1993, 1994, 1996, 1997, 2003, 2007 (* joint winners)

**European Cup/Champions League:** 1968, 1999, 2008

**European Super Cup:** 1991

**World Club Championship:** 1999

## RECORDS

### All-time top appearance makers

| | | |
|---|---|---|
| 1. | Ryan Giggs (1991- ) | 759 |
| 2. | Sir Bobby Charlton (1956-73) | 758 |
| 3. | Bill Foulkes (1952-70) | 688 |
| 4. | Paul Scholes (1994- ) | 570 |
| 5. | Gary Neville (1992- ) | 541 |
| 6. | Alex Stepney (1966-78) | 539 |
| 7. | Tony Dunne (1960-73) | 535 |
| 8. | Denis Irwin (1990-2002) | 529 |
| 9. | Joe Spence (1919-33) | 510 |
| 10. | Arthur Albiston (1974-88) | 485 |

### Most Premiership goals

| | | |
|---|---|---|
| 1. | Ryan Giggs (1991- ) | 96 |
| 2. | Paul Scholes (1994- ) | 96 |
| 3. | Ruud van Nistelrooy (2001-06) | 95 |
| 4. | Andy Cole (1995-2001) | 93 |
| 5. | Ole Gunnar Solskjaer (1996-2007) | 91 |

### Most goals in Europe

| | | |
|---|---|---|
| 1. | Ruud van Nistelrooy (2001-06) | 38 |
| 2. | Denis Law (1962-73) | 28 |
| 3. | Ryan Giggs (1991- ) | 25 |
| 4. | Paul Scholes (1994- ) | 23 |
| 5. | Bobby Charlton (1956-73) | 22 |

### Most FA Cup goals

| | | |
|---|---|---|
| 1. | Denis Law (1962-73) | 34 |
| 2. | Jack Rowley (1937-55) | 26 |
| 3. | George Best (1963-74) | 21 |
| 4. | Stan Pearson (1937-54) | 21 |
| 5. | Bobby Charlton (1956-73) | 19 |

### Record home attendances

82,771*, 29th January 1949, Manchester United 1 Bradford Park Avenue 1 (FA Cup 4th rd)

81,962*, 17th January 1948, Manchester United 1 Arsenal 1 (Division One)

81,565*, 12th February 1949, Manchester United 8 Yeovil 0 (FA Cup 5th rd)

76,098, 31st March 2007, Manchester United 4 Blackburn 1 (Premiership)

76,073, 13th January 2007, Manchester United 3 Aston Villa 1 (Premiership)

* Home matches played at Maine Road following wartime bomb damage to Old Trafford

### Most substitute appearances

| | |
|---|---|
| Ole Gunnar Solskjaer (1996-2007) | 150 |
| Paul Scholes (1994- ) | 96 |
| Ryan Giggs (1991- ) | 90 |
| Phil Neville (1994-2005) | 85 |
| Nicky Butt (1992-2004) | 80 |

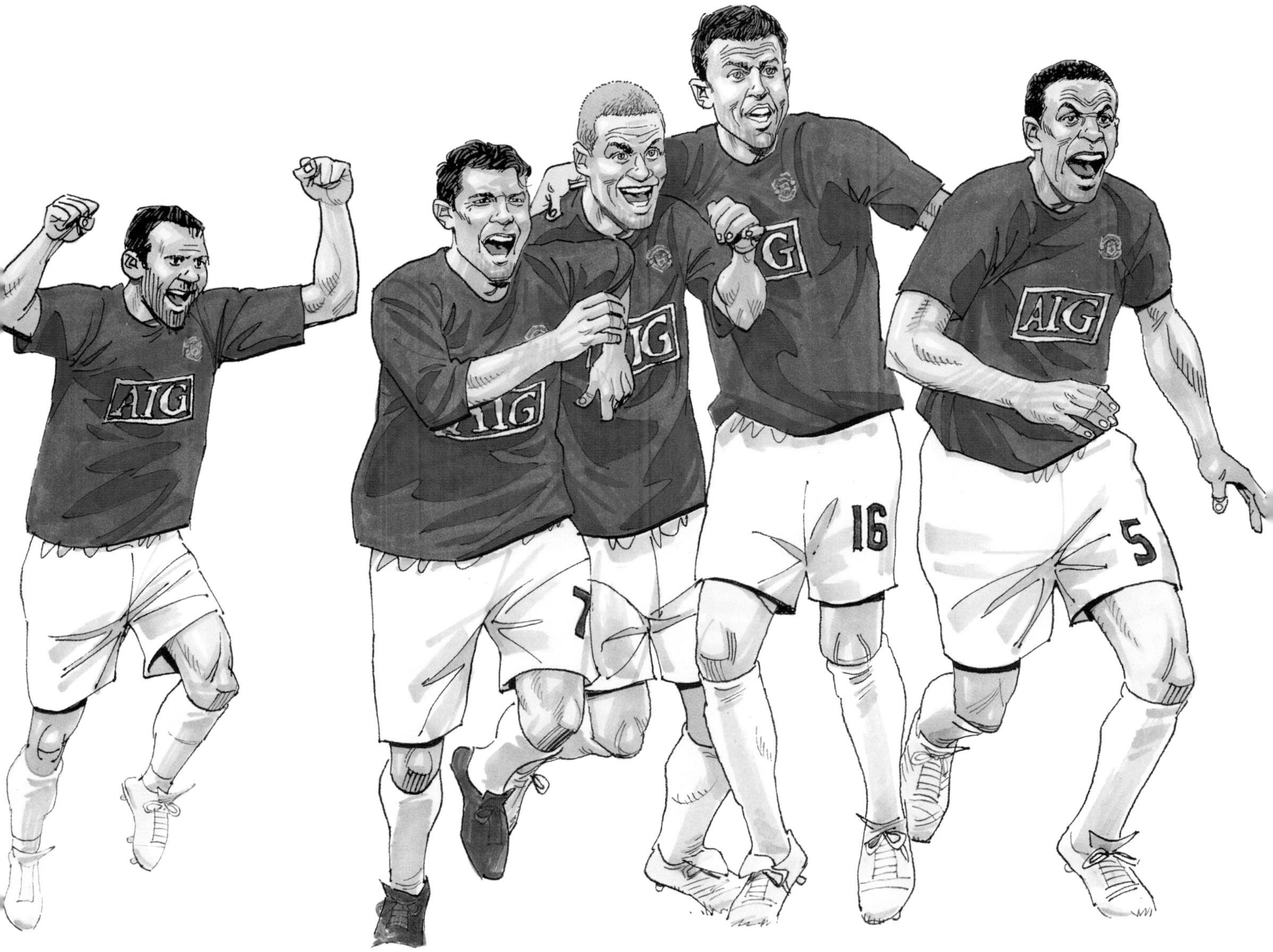
AIG
AIG
AIG
AIG
AIG
16
5

Published by Vision Sports Publishing 2008

Vision Sports Publishing
2 Coombe Gardens
London
SW20 0QU

**www.visionsp.co.uk**

ISBN 13: 978-1-905326-39-6

Art and script: Bob Bond
Cover design: Neal Cobourne
Editor: Jim Drewett

Printed and bound in China by L-rex Printing Co. Ltd

Product Concept: **Ed Chatelier Edge Group**, The Creative Art and literary Group who originated the concept of Soccer Comic Histories including Liverpool, Man United, Newcastle, Everton etc. Also behind The Manga Bible (Hodders), Lion Graphic Bible (Lion) , Yun the Heavenly Man (Monarch) Godspeed  Kurt Cobain Graphic Bio (Omnibus) and Terror rest Prayer (Highland Books) etc.

Contact edgesword@yahoo.com   tel: 07905 060 775
www.edgeart.bravehost.com

A range of high quality merchandise featuring Manchester United  past and present player caricatures drawn by this book's illustrator, Bob Bond, are available to purchase online at www.footielegends.com or for eBay members from www.stores. ebay.co.uk/Footie-Legends.An extensive range of framed or un-framed prints including individual player caricatures, team groups, montages and posters can be purchased along with high quality, 100 per cent UK made, superb bone china tankards and coffee mugs, glass paperweights, greetings cards and a range of smaller items. Excellent as gift ideas or as quality items to add to your personal collection of Manchester United memorabilia.